Maldives

& Islands of the East Indian Ocean
a travel survival kit

Robert Willox

Maldives & Islands of the East Indian Ocean - a travel survival kit
    1st edition

Published by
    Lonely Planet Publications
    Head Office: PO Box 617, Hawthorn, Victoria 3122, Australia
    US Office: PO Box 2001A, Berkeley, CA 94702, USA

Printed by
    Colorcraft, Hong Kong

Photographs by
    Hassan Maniku (HM)
    Robbi Newman, World Expeditions (RN)
    Paul Steel, World Expeditions (PS)
    Robert Willox (RW)
    Front cover: Sea shore, Maldives (RW)

Back cover quote: *Los Angeles Times* © 1989.
    Used with permission.

Published
    January 1990

National Library of Australia Cataloguing in Publication Data

Willox, Robert.
    Maldives & islands of the East Indian Ocean, a travel
    survival kit.

    Includes index.
    ISBN 0 86442 084 6.

    1. Maldives – Description and travel – Guide-books. 2.
    Islands of the East Indian Ocean – Description and travel –
    1981 – – Guide-books. I. Title.

    915.49'504

text ©Lonely Planet 1989
maps ©Lonely Planet 1989
photos ©photographers as indicated 1989

Robert Willox

Robert Willox is a Scottish Highlander by birth and by nature, although he gets on reasonably well with the English. For the past eight years, however, he has made Australia his home.

A journalist since leaving school, Bob has worked for newspapers in England, Scotland, Northern Ireland and, most recently, in Australia for the *Sydney Morning Herald*. In between newspapers, he has enjoyed stints as a philosophy graduate, a Royal Marine officer, an Antarctic expeditioner, a professional actor and an author. He wrote his first book, at the age of 19, about the German bandleader James Last. But don't let that put you off; he now likes Mantovani.

Bob had not written much about his extensive travels until he crossed paths with Lonely Planet. Although his main connection with the Indian Ocean is City Beach in Perth, Western Australia, he is also the author of two other LP travel survival kits: *Mauritius, Réunion & Seychelles* and *Madagascar & Comoros*.

From the Author

With thanks to Ali Waheed, Mohammed Arif, Adam and Hassan Maniku, Allison Phillips, Alimatha Resort, Singapore Airlines, the Maldives Departments of Information and Tourism, and the Territories Branch of the Australian Department of Arts, Sport, Environment, Tourism and Territories in Canberra. None of them should be held accountable in any way for what I have written.

This book is dedicated to Janet.

Thanks also to: Michelle de Kretzer, James Lyon and Lyn McGaurr for proofreading, and Tricia Giles for additional typesetting.

A Warning & a Request

Things change – prices go up, schedules change, good places go bad and bad places go bankrupt – nothing stays the same. So if you find things better or worse, recently opened or long since closed, please write and tell us and help make the next edition better!

Your letters will be used to help update future editions and, where possible, important changes will also be included as a Stop Press section in reprints.

All information is greatly appreciated and the best letters will receive a free copy of the next edition, or any other Lonely Planet book of your choice.

Lonely Planet Credits

Editors	Lindy Cameron
	Sue Mitra
Maps & cover design	Greg Herriman
Design & illustrations	David Windle
Typesetting	Gaylene Miller
	Ann Jeffree

Contents

Introduction

The title 'Maldives & Islands of the East Indian Ocean' covers a lot of territory, or rather a lot of ocean. We're actually dealing with well over 2000 tiny islands sweeping down between two almost parallel lines from either side of India and Sri Lanka for about 1800 km into the Indian Ocean. So there's lots of sea but not much ground; and what land there is looks like it has been shattered into thousands of tiny bits.

There are no wonderful cities or towns, no great edifices, events or rail journeys, and, like the land, the wildlife is limited. More significantly, government restrictions make contact with the local people difficult. So you'd better like the sea because you'll be seeing a lot of it, whether

you choose to simply lie beside it or get right into it and join the marine life.

Seasoned seafarers and experienced divers will already have their favoured maps and guides to this ocean and while this book, hopefully, will be added to their collections it is mainly for the landlubbers, those travellers venturing onto the myriad islands. It concentrates on the bits of land scattered over this part of the Indian Ocean, covering enough pieces of the jigsaw to give you an idea of the overall picture.

There are, not surprisingly, many similarities between the islands, giving the tourist in search of paradise a wide choice of deserted, palm-fringed beaches and coral reefs. However, there are still

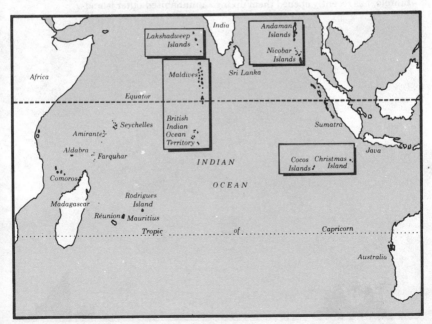

enough differences to appeal to a variety of interests. For a start, the islands are shared by five nations and even more cultures, ranging from the primitive to the most advanced.

By far the largest conglomeration of islands and atolls, and the main destination of tourists, is the independent Republic of Maldives, to the south-west of Sri Lanka.

The Maldives is a nation of islands, rather than an island nation. There are about 1190 of them, little ones, stretching for over 750 km across the equator. This makes for a strange and fascinating country, although much of it is overlooked by most package visitors who are confined to one of the 59 island resorts, often without meeting an actual Maldivian. If you have been packaged, this book will at least tell you what you are missing.

North of the Maldives run the score of Lakshadweep Islands. They belong to India which, following the Maldivian example, has recently opened them up to foreigners. India has also opened up the considerably larger group of Andaman and Nicobar islands in the Bay of Bengal, although thankfully not to the extent of permitting contact with perhaps the world's most isolated and primitive tribes.

The Andaman and Nicobar islands are actually a geographical progression of rainforested Sumatra, but if we skip the Indonesian islands (leaving them to another LP guide), we come to the remote Christmas and Cocos islands, run by Australia and populated largely by people of Chinese-Malay descent. Christmas Island is high, volcanic and forested; Cocos is a flat, coral atoll.

Across 1500 km of empty ocean to the west are the Chagos Islands, owned by the UK and leased to the US for defence (or attack!) purposes. Contact with this 'tribe' is also forbidden, but the authorities turn a blind eye to yachties visiting the uninhabited outer islands.

Facts for the Visitor

VISAS

Try to get all the visas you think you may need before you leave home. It is easier, quicker and cheaper. Bring four to six extra passport photographs for possible visa extensions and any other applications, say for permits.

MONEY

Travellers' cheques are best taken out in US dollars for all countries, although the UK pound, German mark and French franc are also OK. Other major currencies are acceptable. Credit cards are accepted in the Maldives.

COSTS

You can survive on a low budget on the Indian islands, but not in the Maldives, unless you stay on the capital island Male where you can survive on US$20 a day.

Resorts are expensive on a day to day basis and generally cheaper as a package holiday, although there may be some daily bargains in the low season from May to October.

Accommodation and meals for visitors on the Australian islands, Cocos and Christmas, are provided by the island authorities at around A$65 a day for full board. The only alternative is a package holiday to Cocos from Perth, Western Australia.

HEALTH

In this part of the world the sun is the greatest general threat to your wellbeing. Bring a good sun blocking lotion with you as the cost of sun lotions is high and the choice limited. You can tan easily and well within a week to 10 days, using a high-protection cream.

Don't underestimate the effects of the sun, even if you think you know your tolerance level. Take it easy to begin with when you go about exposing yourself to the fiery elements. It's very easy to get badly burnt even when it's overcast. It's a good idea to wear a hat of some kind and sunglasses.

Drink plenty of liquids and keep salt intake up to replace that lost through perspiration.

Vaccinations

Vaccinations for hepatitis, tetanus, cholera, polio and typhoid should be considered if you are planning to go bush or travel around the region for a long period of time. Your government health department will advise you on which vaccinations are currently recommended. The only vaccination required for entry to the Maldives and other islands in this book is the jab for yellow fever – if you have just been to a potentially infected area.

Malaria

Malaria has 'officially' been wiped out in the Maldives. There are, however, still cases of the disease even if the government prefers to register them as something else.

So you should still take a course of malaria tablets – just in case; and it's a must if you're travelling around the other island groups.

There are some islands in the Indian Ocean where the chloroquine-resistant malarial strains exist. Chloroquine should still be taken, but a weekly dose of Maloprim or a daily dose of Proguanil should also be taken. You have to start your course of malaria tablets two weeks before you enter a malarial area and continue for up to six weeks after you leave.

Warning: Fansidar is no longer recommended as a prophylactic.

Mosquito coils or a non-aerosol repellent are useful in keeping the vicious brutes at bay.

9

Common Ailments

The Traveller's Curse The bane of nearly every traveller's life is the one you can do the least about. Called a variety of names from Delhi-belly to the Pharaoh's Curse or Montezuma's Revenge, depending on where you happen to be, it is more commonly known as diarrhoea.

If you do have an attack of diarrhoea the best way to treat it, however, is with no drugs. It's probably just your body's way of adjusting to a new environment and different food, so the most important thing to do is replenish your bodily fluids to avoid dehydration. A diet of bland foods such as rice, bread and weak tea is a good treatment.

The are a few stop-gap measures, that will stem the flow if absolutely necessary; if you have to travel for instance. Lomotil or imodium can be used to bring relief from the symptoms; they do not, however, cure the problem.

If you also have a fever, then your ailment might be something more serious, like amoebic dysentery, in which case you should see a doctor.

Cuts All cuts, no matter how minor, should be treated seriously and carefully if you're travelling in a tropical climate. Put mercurochrome on any cut or scratch, keep the wound clean and dry and check for any sign of infection. Deep or large cuts should be treated with antibiotic powder. (Cream is not as effective as the wound should be kept dry.) Avoid bandages or bandaids unless absolutely necessary.

Travel Insurance

It is a good idea to take out travel insurance. Look at a few policies to see what you will be covered for; some are better than others for certain activities, like diving or motor cycling. Make sure you're adequately covered for medical expenses, for the cost of getting home for treatment, life insurance and baggage insurance. Check the fine print!

Medical Kit

Carry a basic first aid kit with an antiseptic agent (Dettol), antibiotic powder and cream, bandaids, a gauze bandage, small scissors, burn cream and insect repellent.

Don't forget any medication you're already taking, contraceptive pills or condoms if necessary, and women should bring a sufficient supply of tampons.

Bring seasickness pills if you're a bad sailor, as you will probably spend a lot of time on the water travelling between local islands.

DANGERS & ANNOYANCES

Crime is not rife on any island, but there are plenty of thieves about.

Marine Dangers

Unless you know about marine life, don't touch the coral, shells or fish – some of them sting, cut and occasionally kill. Don't swim or let yourself drift too far away from the boat or shore in case you get caught in a strong current. Keep away from the surf breaking on the reef edge, or anywhere else for that matter. One big wave and you could be fish fodder. Sharks are the least of your worries.

Security

A waterproof money belt or kidney pouch for your passport, flight tickets and travellers' cheques is worth considering. Use a day backpack to carry the bits and pieces you'll need for the day, as well as your camera and valuables.

Don't leave vital documents, money or valuables in your room or in your suitcase while travelling. Don't sleep with an open window which is accessible from the outside, or with the door open or unlocked. I was robbed on a Maldivian island by a bedroom prowler. He got my daypack with my camera in it, but, as I was sleeping with my money belt on, all was far from lost.

FILM & PHOTOGRAPHY

Film will be much more expensive than that which you can buy duty free before you leave home, so stock up. Only Male and some of the resorts in the Maldives have reasonable photographic and processing shops. Remember also to take spare batteries for cameras and flash units.

If you are a reasonably knowledgeable photographer, I need only remind you about the heat, humidity, very fine sand, tropical sunlight, equatorial shadows and the great opportunities for underwater photography. If you are not, then this may be a case of the blind leading the blind. There are heaps of books on photography but one of the best all-rounders is *The New 35mm Photographer's Handbook* by Julian Calder & John Garrett (Pan)

Use Kodachrome 25 or 64 transparency (slide) film, rather than Ektachrome. The cost of the film usually includes processing and you can mail the rolls back to the labs in the envelopes provided. Rewrap the package to disguise it and send it registered if you don't trust the post. Kodacolor 100 film is the most popular print film and is fine for most general photography in the tropics.

Don't leave your camera in direct sunlight, keep it protected from dust and sand, and don't store used film for long in the humid conditions as it will fade.

The best times to take photographs on sunny days are the first two hours after sunrise and the last two before sunset. This brings out the best colours. At other times, the harsh sunlight and glare washes everything out, though you can use filters to counter the glare.

Photographing people, particularly dark-skinned people, requires more skill than snapping landscapes. Make sure you take the light reading from the subject's face, not the background. It also requires more patience and politeness. Many islanders, particularly the older Muslims and Hindus, are offended or frightened by snap-happy intruders. You should always ask first, ingratiate yourself, or snap discreetly from a distance.

Don't take photographs of airports or anything that looks like either police or military equipment or property.

Finally, if you are worried about X-ray security machines at airports ruining your film, despite assurances that they won't, simply remove your camera and film stock from your luggage and take it through separately for inspection.

BOOKS

If you intend to do a lot of reading, just bring a few paperbacks with you as you'll probably be able to swap them later with other travellers. In preparation for shoestring travelling, as opposed to package tripping, read *The Tropical Traveller* by John Hatt (Pan, 1982).

If you're after detailed info on the multicoloured wonders of the deep, refer directly to either *A Field Guide to the Coral Reef Fish of the Indian & West Pacific Oceans* by R H Carcasson (Collins, London, 1977), or *A Guide to Common Reef Fish of the Western Indian Ocean* by K R Bock (Macmillan, London, 1987).

If you're planning a more extensive exploration of the Indian Ocean, Lonely Planet has two other guide books to the region: *Madagascar & Comoros* and *Mauritius, Réunion & Seychelles*.

WHAT TO BRING
Clothes

Keep clothing light and in cotton wherever possible. This particularly applies to your socks if you intend to do lots of walking.

Anything as formal as a suit is unnecessary, but it's good to have a smart pair of trousers and shirt or dress/skirt and shoes for dinners out. Such an outfit can also help at customs and immigration, when entering or leaving a country. If nothing else, it makes you feel more respectable, and therefore respected, than you would in shorts, T-shirt and thongs.

Make sure you have adequate protection from the sun. Bring a hat, sunglasses and an appropriate-strength sun cream. At the other extreme, a light wrap-up plastic cape or mac will stop a downpour from ruining the odd day or week. It's a must during the wet season.

It does actually cool down a bit at night but not enough to need woolly blankets and thick jumpers.

Basic Kit

If you're going to be roughing it away from the resort accommodation and living with islanders or in guest houses, you should bring a torch with spare batteries, toilet paper, a small mirror (shiny metal is best), a Swiss Army knife or the like, a first aid kit (see the Health section), a sewing kit with safety pins, sticky tape and a small padlock for locking rooms or luggage.

Also, remember to take precautions to keep your camera equipment and personal gear dry. Pack everything in plastic bags before you leave home.

All this doesn't add up to much extra weight. If you're looking to lighten your load, keep your towels thin.

ACTIVITIES
Diving

The Maldives is a top diving spot, said to be second-best in the world after the Red Sea. Most tourists go to the Maldives for

that reason, or return having been converted to the pursuit.

For those new to diving, most of the instructors and schools in this region are members of the US-based Professional Association of Diving Instructors (PADI) and provide safety and tuition up to that standard. The other major organisation is FAUI.

If the diving school you choose does not possess either of these qualifications, then you may be taking a grave risk with instruction and equipment.

In addition, your ability, health and qualifications should be checked before any operator sells you courses or takes you out on an introductory dive. This is done through a check-out in the swimming pool or lagoon. All beginners must be able to swim at least 200 metres before proceeding.

Snorkelling

For the little paddlers, like me, who are content with snorkelling, watch out for sunburn, especially on your back. Wear a light T-shirt or use a water-resistant sunblock cream or lotion.

Conservation Note

Don't buy anything made out of turtleshell or permanently remove any shells from the beach. Stocks of turtles and shells have been cleared in many areas, or are otherwise endangered. No government is doing much about it, so please don't contribute to the problems.

Getting There

A yacht, a big yacht, is the best way to get to and around this region, although there are still many restrictions in force as to where you can visit by boat. Refer to the Getting There sections for each island group for costs and details of air and sea travel.

There are no cruise lines plying the ocean waves of this region, but there are plenty of airlines.

Because of its large tourism industry there are many regular air services to the Maldives (Male is the country's only port of entry), supplemented by scores of charter services during the high season.

Colombo in Sri Lanka, Trivandrum in south-west India, and Singapore are the main departure points for the Maldives. There are also weekly flights to the Maldives from Karachi in Pakistan, Dubai in Bahrain and Kathmandu in Nepal.

Christmas Island and the Cocos group share the same Australian government-chartered air service. To get to either you must fly from Perth or Singapore.

The Lakshadweep, Andaman and Nicobar islands can only be reached via India. Indian Airlines has four flights a week between Port Blair in the Andamans, and Madras (Rs 1255) or Calcutta (Rs 1245). You'll need to book well ahead as flights are often booked up weeks in advance. There are also regular boat services from Madras and Calcutta and the Shipping Corporation of India puts out a schedule about every three months. Foreigners are required to travel 1st or 2nd class.

The Chagos Islands are accessible only by boat except for the US military base on Diego Garcia which is completely off limits to civilians anyway.

There are no direct air or sea links between Maldives and any of the other islands groups covered in the book.

From UK & Europe

There are direct regular weekly services to the Maldives from London, Amsterdam, Brussels and Zurich. Charter flights are mostly in the high season (November to April) from London, Rome, Milan, Vienna, Zurich, Dusseldorf, Munich and Frankfurt.

For Lakshadweep, Andaman and Nicobar islands, fly first to Bombay, Calcutta or Madras.

For Cocos and Christmas, you must fly via Australia or Singapore.

From Australia

There are no direct flights from Australia to the Maldives. The quickest, simplest way is by Singapore Airlines via Singapore, but it may be cheaper to fly to Colombo with Air Lanka.

There is a regular Tuesday flight from Perth to Cocos and Christmas.

From USA

Again, there are no direct air services to the Indian Ocean. Travellers must get to Europe or Asia first.

Facts about the Country

More than 114,000 people are attracted to the Maldives each year by images of 'the last paradise on earth'. About 90% of the visitors go to resorts on seven to 14-day packages and 90% of them go diving. Going to the Maldives and not diving is like going to the Himalaya and not trekking or going to Singapore and not shopping.

The Maldives is an exhilarating but expensive place to visit. The authorities have put a stop to visitors finding any cheaper alternatives to the resorts, and that makes it difficult for the low-budget traveller. Islands are now out of bounds to visitors, except for the resorts and the capital, Male. You can no longer breeze in for a spot of island-hopping or drop out on a deserted island.

The government restrictions are to prevent visitors 'corrupting' the local Muslim life style and undercutting the tourist industry. Sadly, they also prevent anyone getting to know the Maldives and its people properly.

The paradise images that woo tourists are by no means misleading, but the first fact that most people are surprised to learn about the Maldives is that it is an independent Islamic country, not just a cluster of romantic, deserted islands off the coast of India, Sri Lanka or 'somewhere like that'. Indeed, the Republic of Maldives is a *very* independent nation. It has been looking after itself longer than most other small nations, and has a history, culture and language all of its own.

Another surprising fact is the fragmented and scattered nature of this nation's geography. It is made up of, approximately, 1190 tiny islands, none of which are higher than a few metres above sea level. This makes travelling difficult, or at least challenging.

Despair not, however, there are ways of getting around the country, though you'd better visit soon. If predicted consequences of the greenhouse effect become a reality, the Maldives will be under threat of extinction from rising sea levels; the country could vanish completely by the year 2020.

HISTORY

The history of the Maldives can be divided into two stages – before and after the conversion to Islam in 1153 AD.

The second stage is well documented through a series of sultanic dynasties to the recent birth and re-birth of the republic. The pre-Muslim period, however, is full of hazy, heroic myth mixed with conjectures based on archaeological discoveries.

The Muslim authorities are not interested in what went on before Islam and tend to use the myths of legendary queens and princes as biblical stories to support the ensuing conversion.

It was foreign archaeologists such as H C P Bell early this century and, more recently, Kon-Tiki explorer Thor Heyerdahl who have attempted to explain the tangible, although insubstantial, remains of early civilisations.

Early Days

The first settlers probably arrived in the uninhabited archipelago from Ceylon (Sri Lanka) and southern India, not later than 500 BC.

Thor Heyerdahl, however, explores the theory that the existence of the Maldives was well known long before that. Rather than being isolated or ignored they were, from around 2000 BC onwards, at the trading crossroads of several ancient maritime nations.

He believes the ancient Egyptians, Romans, Mesopotamians and Indus Valley traders all called by at one time or another. Which ones settled to become

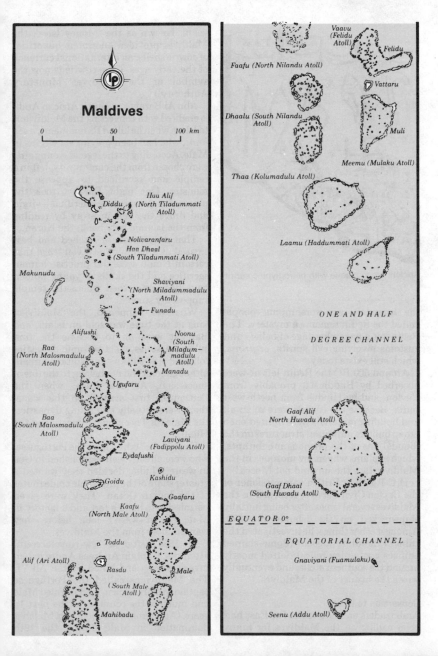

Ancient stone plaque with heiroglyphic script

years. Known as the 'Money Isles', the Maldives provided enormous quantities of cowrie shells, an international currency of the early ages. (The cowrie is now the symbol of the Maldives Monetary Authority.)

Abu Al Barakat, a North African Arab, is credited with converting the Maldivians to Islam when he killed Rannamaari, a sea *jinni*, who had been preying on virgins in Male. According to the legend, young girls were chosen from the community, left in a temple and sacrificed to appease the monster. One night Barakat took the place of a prospective sacrificial virgin and drove the demon away by reading from the Islamic holy book, the Koran.

That may seem far-fetched and best treated as a parable until you learn that certain Hindu sects did practise human sacrifice and the skulls of young women have been unearthed where the temple supposedly stood.

Whatever happened, the Maldivian king at the time was sold on Islam, and Barakat went on to become the first sultan. A series of six sultanic dynasties followed – 84 sultans and sultanas in all, although some did not belong to the line of succession. At one stage, when the Portuguese first arrived on the scene, there were actually two ruling dynasties, the Male (or Theemuge) dynasty and the Hilali.

Early in the 16th century the Portuguese, who were already well-established in Goa in western India, decided they wanted a greater share of the profitable trade routes of the Indian Ocean. They were given permission to build a fort and a factory in Male but it wasn't long before they wanted more from the Maldives.

In 1558, after a few unsuccessful attempts, Captain Andreas Andre led an invasion army and killed Sultan Ali VI. The Maldivians called the Portuguese captain 'Andiri Andirin' and he ruled Male and much of the country for the next 15 years. (Apart from a few months of Malabar domination in Male during the 18th

the legendary sun-worshipping people called the Redin remains a mystery. The Redin left a pagan heritage of beliefs and customs involving evil spirits, or *jinnis*, which still exists today.

Around 500 BC the Redin left or were absorbed by Buddhists, probably from Ceylon, and by Hindus from north-west India. Because the islands were so small and building materials were limited each group built its important structures on the foundations of the previous inhabitants, which explains why many mosques in the Maldives face the sun and not Mecca!

H C P Bell, a British commissioner of the Ceylon Civil Service, returned to the Maldives several times after being initially shipwrecked on the islands in 1879. Amongst other things, he investigated the ruins of Buddhist *dagobas* (dome-shaped edifices containing relics) dotted mostly around the southern atolls, and eventually wrote the history of the Maldives.

Conversion to Islam

Arab traders en route to the Far East had been calling on the Maldives for many century, this was the only time that another country has occupied the Maldives.)

The brutal Portuguese occupation came to a bloody end in 1573 when Mohammed Thakurufaan, chief of Utheem Island in the northern atoll of Tiladummati, and his two brothers led a commando attack on the Portuguese garrison and slew the lot. Thakurufaan went on to start the next sultanic dynasty, the Utheem. He also introduced coins to replace the cowrie currency. (A memorial centre to commemorate Thakurufaan, the Maldives' greatest hero, was opened on Utheem in November 1986.)

During the next couple of centuries, the Malabar rajas of south India, and to a lesser extent the Portuguese, made frequent attacks on the Maldivian sultans. They didn't succeed in a military sense, but took over trading interests instead.

In the 17th century the Maldives came under the protection of the Dutch rulers of Ceylon. That protection was extended by the British after they took possession of Ceylon in 1796, although it was not formalised for 90 years. Because of the remoteness and unhealthiness of the islands, neither the Dutch nor the British established a colonial administration.

In the 1860s Borah merchants from Bombay were invited to Male to establish warehouses and shops, but it wasn't long before they acquired an almost exclusive monopoly on the foreign trade. The Maldivians feared the Borahs would soon gain complete control of the islands so Sultan Mohammed Mueenuddin II signed an agreement with the British in 1887 which guaranteed the islands' full independence. The Maldives became a British protectorate, in return for defence facilities.

20th Century

The sultanate became an elected position rather than a hereditary one when, in 1932, the Maldives' first constitution was imposed upon Sultan Shamsuddin, who was subsequently deposed. The next sultan, Hasan Nurudin II, abdicated in 1943 and his replacement, the elderly Abdul Majeed Didi, retired to Ceylon (Sri Lanka) leaving the control of the government in the hands of his prime minister, Mohammed Amin Didi.

Amin Didi nationalised the fish export industry, instituted a broad modernisation programme and introduced a total ban on tobacco smoking.

When Ceylon gained independence in 1948 the Maldivians signed a defence pact with the British which gave the latter control of the foreign affairs of the islands but not the right to interfere internally. In return the Maldivians agreed to provide facilities for the British forces for the defence of the islands and of the Commonwealth.

In 1953 the sultanate was abolished and a republic was proclaimed, with Amin Didi as its first president. Didi was too tough too soon however, and the new government was short-lived. Less than a year after he came to power Didi was overthrown and, during a riot over food shortages, was beaten by a mob and died on Kurumba Island. The sultanate was returned, with Mohammed Farid Didi elected as the 94th sultan of the Maldives.

While Britain, the absentee landlord, did not overtly interfere in the running of the country or impose judicial and cultural changes it did secure permission to re-establish its wartime airfield on Gan Island in the southernmost Addu Atoll. In 1956 the Royal Air Force began developing the base as a staging post, employing hundreds of Maldivians, and undertook the resettlement of the Gan islanders. The British were informally granted a 100 year lease of Gan which required them to pay £2000 a year.

When Ibrahim Nasir was elected prime minister in 1957 he immediately called for a review of the agreement with the British on Gan, demanding that the lease be shortened and the annual payment increased.

This was followed by an insurrection against the Maldivian government by the inhabitants of the southern atolls of Addu and Suvadiva (Huvadu), who objected to Nasir's demand that the British cease employing local labour. Undoubtedly influenced by the British presence, they decided to cut ties altogether and form an independent state, electing Abdulla Afif Didi president.

In 1960, however, the Maldivian government officially granted the British the use of Gan and other facilities in Addu Atoll for 30 years (effective from December 1956) in return for the payment of £100,000 a year and a grant of £750,000 to finance specific development projects over a period of years.

In 1962, Nasir sent gunboats from Male to quash the rebellion in the southern atolls. Afif fled to the Seychelles, then a British colony, while other leaders were banished to various islands in the Maldives.

In 1965 Britain recognised the islands as a completely sovereign and independent state, and ceased to be responsible for their defence (although it retained the use of Gan and continued to pay rent until 1976). The Maldives were granted independence on 26 July 1965 and later became a member of the United Nations.

Following a referendum in 1968 the sultanate was again abolished, Sultan Majeed Didi retired to Ceylon and a new republic was inaugurated. Nasir was elected president.

Nasir ruled for 10 years, seemingly becoming more autocratic each year. The Sri Lankan market for the Maldives' biggest export, dried fish, collapsed in 1972. Fortunately that was the year the tourist industry was born with the opening of Kurumba and Bandos resorts.

Unfortunately, however, the money generated by tourism didn't directly benefit the populace. Prices kept going up and there were revolts, plots and banishments as Nasir clung to power. In response to one protest in 1974 Nasir ordered the police to open fire on a large crowd which had gathered to air their grievances.

In 1978, fearing for his life, Nasir stepped down and skipped across to Singapore reputedly with US$4 million from the Maldivian national coffers.

Former university lecturer and Maldivian ambassador to the United Nations, Maumoon Abdul Gayoom, was elected president in Nasir's place. Gayoom's style of governing was much more open, and he immediately denounced Nasir's regime and banished several of the former president's associates.

In 1980 a coup plot against Gayoom, involving mercenaries, was discovered and more banishments occurred; the list included more of Nasir's cohorts. Extradition proceedings began, for the second time, to have Nasir brought back from Singapore to stand trial for murder and theft. They were unsuccessful.

Gayoom was re-elected in 1983 and has done much to further education, health and industry, particularly tourism. He has also given the tiny country a higher international profile with full membership in the Commonwealth of Nations and the South Asian Regional Co-operation (SARC) group.

His main opposition today comes from Muslim fundamentalists who want to return to a more traditional way of life, and from powerful local business barons whose interests are often said to dictate government decisions.

In January 1986, unable to extradite Nasir, the Maldivian High Court sentenced the ex-president *in absentia* to 25 years banishment.

In September 1988, the 51-year-old Gayoom was re-elected for a third term as president although, as the only candidate, it was really a referendum to see if he should continue in office for another five years. More than 96% of the people voted 'yes'.

Gayoom's sense of security was shattered only a month later. A group of disaffected Maldivian businessmen attempted a coup employing about 400 Sri Lankan Tamil mercenaries. Half of these soldiers infiltrated Male as visitors, while the rest landed by boat. The mercenaries took the airport on Hulhule Island and several key installations on Male, but failed to capture the National Security Guard headquarters.

More than 1600 Indian paratroopers, immediately dispatched by Prime Minister Rajiv Gandhi, ended further gains by the invaders who then fled by boat towards Sri Lanka. They took 27 hostages and left 14 people dead and 40 wounded. No tourists were affected.

The mercenaries were later caught by an Indian frigate 100 km from the Sri Lankan coast. According to authorities, four hostages were found dead and three were missing.

Sixty of the mercenaries were returned to the Maldives for trial in July 1989. Several were sentenced to death. (The last death sentence to be carried out in the Maldives was in 1951.)

Ibrahim Nasir has denied any involvement in the coup attempt. The assault was headed by Abdulla Luthufi, a former Maldivian exporter of tropical fish, who had lived in Sri Lanka since 1985.

GEOGRAPHY

The Maldives are a chain of about 2000 small, low-lying coral islands grouped in clusters, or atolls, about 600 km south-west of Sri Lanka. The word 'atoll' actually derives from the Maldivian word *atolu*.

With a total land area of 298 square km, the 26 atolls stretch out across the equator in a thin strip 754 km long and 118 km wide. There are no hills or rivers in the Maldives as none of the islands rises more than three metres above sea level or is longer than eight km; though some of the atolls measure up to 40 km long and 20 km wide.

Just how many islands make up the Maldives has never been conclusively determined. Estimates throughout history have ranged from 1300 to 13,000. The government says there are 1190 islands, of which only 202 are inhabited. To further confuse the issue, there are 59 resort islands which, in most cases, are classed as 'uninhabited by Maldivians'.

Some of the islands are simply tiny palm-covered coral sandbanks that take 10 minutes to walk around, while larger islands are covered with bamboo, banyan, mangroves and towering coconut palms.

Built of coral on the peaks of an ancient submerged volcanic mountain range, and protected from the open ocean and the destructive effects of monsoons by barrier reefs, the Maldive atolls have brilliant white sand beaches surrounded by deep, crystal clear lagoons.

The protective reefs may not be enough, however, to save the Maldives from the disaster which scientific experts warn will befall the islands in the not too distant future. They fear the whole chain of atolls could be submerged within 30 years by the rising sea levels caused by the greenhouse effect. Island water supplies could run out as early as 1992 and already strong tidal waves have left a trail of destruction on several islands.

President Gayoom made an impassioned plea for help to the 1987 Commonwealth Heads of Government conference. The problem is now one of many receiving international attention.

Coral Atolls

A coral reef or garden is not, as many people believe, formed of multi-coloured marine plants. It is rather, a living colony of coral polyps, which are tiny tentacled creatures that feed on plankton.

These coral polyps, which are related to both the jellyfish and the sea anemone, are invertebrates with sacklike bodies and calcerous or horny skeletons. After extracting calcium deposits from the water around them, these polyps excrete tiny cup-shaped limestone skeletons.

A coral reef is the rock-like aggregation of millions of these animals or their skeletons. Only the outer layer of coral is alive. As polyps reproduce and die, the new polyps attach themselves in successive layers to the skeletons already in place.

Charles Darwin was the first to put forward the theory that atolls develop from coral growth which has built up around the edges of a submerged volcanic mountain peak.

In a scenario played out over hundreds of thousands of years, coral first builds up around the shores of a volcanic land mass producing a fringing reef. Then, when the island (often simply the exposed peak of a submarine mountain) begins slowly to sink, the coral continues to grow upwards at about the same rate.

This forms a barrier reef which is separated from the shore of the sinking island by a lagoon. By the time the island is completely submerged, the coral growth has become the base for an atoll, circling the place where the volcanic land mass or mountain used to be.

As the centuries pass, sand and debris accumulate on the higher parts of the reef and vegetation eventually takes root, creating islands. The classic atoll shape is roughly oval, incorporating these islands of coral rubble and enclosing others in deep-water lagoons. There are usually breaks in the reef rim large enough for boats to enter the sheltered lagoon.

CLIMATE

The year is divided into two monsoons which also determine the high and low tourist seasons. The north-east monsoon lasts from the beginning of December to the end of March and marks the high season and high prices. February is the driest and busiest month – the one to avoid if you are travelling.

The wetter south-west monsoon, from the end of April to the end of October,

brings the worst weather with stronger winds and storms, particularly in June. For a tourist paying US$2000 for an idyllic fortnight holiday, the low season is probably too much of a risk. But the traveller shouldn't balk at it, especially with the prospect of better travel and resort deals.

The temperature ranges between 24°C and 33°C throughout the year, with relatively high humidity. Continual sea breezes keep the air moving and make life quite bearable, but you can't always count on the weather patterns. When I was there at the height of the dry season, it rained continuously over the whole country for more than a week. In Male, you didn't go out for a walk, you went out for a wade. In recent years, November has been the wettest month by far, followed by May.

FLORA & FAUNA

Plants and animals are not exactly the Maldives' main drawcards, except of course for the amazing wildlife under the sea. The vegetation ranges from thick to sparse to none at all and, while there are no extensive tropical jungles, there are areas of rainforest.

The islands have sandy beaches, lagoons, mangroves, and luxuriant stands of breadfruit trees, banyans, bamboo, pandanus, banana, tropical vines and, naturally, the ubiquitous coconut palm.

Sweet potatoes, yams, taro plants and millet are grown. No crop is rich or plentiful, except perhaps on the atoll-island of Fuamulaku in the extreme south, where citrus fruits and pineapples grow.

Animals are few and far between, although goats, chickens and the occasional cow are kept.

Giant fruit bats or flying foxes are common to many islands; you'll see them cruising past at dusk. They are not eaten here as they are in the Seychelles. There are pet cats but no dogs, and you may come across a rat or two. (By the way, those who have visited Bali will appreciate the irony in the Maldivian word for dog – *kuta*!)

The mosquito population varies from island to island but tends not to be too bothersome in Male and the villages. Only occasionally will you encounter other insects, lizards and creepy-crawlies; none of which are supposed to be dangerous. On the other hand, explorer Thor Heyerdahl tells how one of his expeditioners nearly died after receiving a bite on the leg, which he believed was delivered by a large centipede.

There are more than 700 species of fish in the Indian Ocean, most of which have been seen by diving enthusiasts in the Maldives, which makes the islands one of the best natural aquariums in the world.

You don't even need to be a diver to make the most of the Maldives' underwater tourist attraction. A snorkel, flippers and a few short strokes from the beach will take you into a world of extraordinary beauty where you can swim amongst amazing multi-coloured reef fish, skipjack tuna and coral gardens. While divers marvel at half of the species, the locals eat the other half.

GOVERNMENT

The Maldivian parliament, the *Majlis*, or Citizens' Council, has 48 members. Male, which is the capital island, and each of the atolls has two elected representatives. The president chooses the remaining eight parliamentary representatives; has the power to appoint or dismiss cabinet ministers; and appoints all judges, who administer justice under the tenets of Islam.

The president is nominated by the Majlis and the appointment is put to a national referendum. There is no choice of candidates and to vote against the candidate would be to vote against the chosen religious, as well as military and political leader. Gayoom got in with 98% of the vote. Elections take place every five years.

National Emblem of the Maldives

Local government, of the 19 administrative atolls, is in the hands of each *atolu verin*, or atoll chief. The *gazi* is the religious head of the atoll and joins the atoll chief in legal matters.

ECONOMY

The Maldives has a developing economy based on fishing, tourism and shipping, but it is still one of the poorest countries in the world.

Most of the population survive outside the money-based economy, subsisting on fishing, coconut gathering and the growing of millet, corn, yams and sorghum. Cropland is minimal and scattered over many small islands.

Despite efforts to increase agricultural output, nearly all the food for the increasing population has to be imported. The government plans to raise import taxes on fruits and vegetables to get people to grow more of their own.

With the exception of the national shipping line and the tuna canning factory, industry in the Maldives is mostly of the cottage or handcraft type, and includes boatbuilding, and the making of coconut oil, coir (coconut-husk fibre) and coir products such as rope and matting. Local craft industries are encouraged to expand with assistance from the United Nations Development Programme (UNDP).

Fishing, the traditional base of the economy, employs almost 40% of the labour force and accounts for about 40% of the earnings received from exports. Skipjack tuna is the principal catch, followed by yellowfin, little tuna and frigate mackerel, as well as reef fish such as sharks.

The national shipping line, Maldives Shipping Ltd (MSL), forms the basis of the country's second largest commercial industry.

The fishing industry was dealt a blow in 1972 when the rich Sri Lankan market for 'Maldive Fish' (smoked and dried skipjack tuna) collapsed. The government, however, knuckled down and started mechanising the fishing fleet of *dhonis* and improving navigational aids, although the actual fishing is still done by the simple pole and line method.

The government took control of a tuna-canning factory in Laviyani atoll, and export markets for canned, frozen and salted fish were opened in Japan, Korea, Singapore and some European countries.

Towards the end of 1981, a glut of tuna on the international market sent the price plummeting. At the same time there was a glut of shipping and freight prices crashed. To make matters worse the Gulf War between Iraq and Iran hit the Maldives shipping industry, cutting trade and reducing Maldives Shipping Ltd by two-thirds.

The country had to borrow large sums of money and ask for aid, which they managed to get without having to align themselves with a superpower. Instead of accepting an offer from either the Russians or Americans, who had both been after Gan as a military base, the Maldives turned the former RAF base over to two Hong Kong garment manufacturers and the Maldives State Trading Organisation.

The great advantage for the garment firms is that clothing made in the Maldives avoids western quota restrictions on imports from Hong Kong. The government continues to try to attract investors with offers like tax incentives for resort developers and no foreign exchange controls.

Indians used to come to the Maldives in droves to buy up foreign goods which were cheaper in Male. But in 1983 the Indian government slashed duty-free allowances for arrivals from Sri Lanka and the Maldives, so these days India has little trade with the islands. In one year, the number of Indian visitors dropped from almost 15,000 to just over 3000, which accounts for the closure of most of the cheap guest houses in Male.

Even though the average income is the equivalent of only a few hundred dollars a year, there are no beggars in the Maldives.

Tourism

It was an Italian tour operator, George Corbin, who saw the tourist potential of the Maldives when he visited the islands in 1972. (Coincidentally, *Corbin* was also the name of a French ship wrecked off Fuladu in Baa Atoll in 1602. It made a castaway of François Pyrard, who wrote an account of his experience among the 'natives'.)

Later the same year, after a promotional tour by travel writers, Kurumba Island was opened as a resort and the Italian tourists took to it like parmesan to bolognaise.

As word spread around Europe, other islands close to Male were turned into resorts. By 1977 there were 11, and six to eight resorts have been added each year since then, bringing the number to 59 at the end of 1989. Tourism is now a US$42 million a year industry and the largest earner of foreign exchange.

Most of the tourists who visit the Maldives are West Germans. Out of 114,000 visitors to the country each year, around 31,000 (27%) come from West Germany, though they're joined by about 20,000 Italians and an increasing number of Japanese. The French, Swiss, British and Australians arrive in roughly equal numbers. Some resorts are used exclusively by Germans or Italians.

All land is state-owned. Initially the uninhabited islands were leased out to shopkeepers, businesspeople and *befalus* (upper class people) for agricultural development. Agricultural leases were bought for less than Rf 1000 (US$143).

Then along came the tour operators, hoteliers and other foreign investors. Once they had approval from the government, they would finance the building and management of the resort and either take the Maldivian lessee on as a partner or pay them Rf 50,000 a year. The government gains from taxes and rents. Maldivians now own and run 34 resorts.

Since North and South Male atolls have been developed, the government is continuing resort expansion into Alif (Ari Atoll).

PEOPLE

There are 198,000 people in the Maldives, 54,000 of whom live in Male. It is thought that the original settlers were Dravidian and Sinhalese people who came from south India and Ceylon. There has also been a great deal of intermarriage and mixing with Arabian and African people.

A distinguishing physical characteristic is the size of the people; Maldivians are generally small of stature. You can tell the difference between the locals and any Indian visitors because the latter are noticeably much bigger.

The most obvious character trait of the Maldivian people is their nonaggressive nature. They laugh a lot and anger is rarely openly expressed. Expatriates in Male will tell you that they have never seen a fight between Maldivians.

That doesn't mean to say they're completely lovable or easily pushed around. One volunteer summed it up when he said violence in Maldivian society was of a psychological, rather than a physical nature; and although the people are openly warm to outsiders, it takes a long time to get over their 'trust threshold'.

You'll find Maldivians don't have a very servile attitude towards visitors. Unlike the Sri Lankans, Indians and Pakistanis, they have no experience with colonialism (except with the RAF on Gan). Outside of Male, Addu and Ari atolls people may not have seen a white person for several years, if at all.

You can address Maldivians by their first or last name. Since so many men are called Mohammed, Hassan or Ali, the surname is more appropriate and, in many cases, the honorary title. *Maniku* is another title used to bestow respect.

The names Manik and Didi belong, by and large, to the *befalu* or upper class, privileged families. At the other end of the scale you have the Giravaru people, the descendants of the early settlers from southern India. They are the Maldives aborigines, treated as inferior, and are fast

disappearing as a tribe though a small community resides in Male. Their island, Giraavaru, is now a tourist resort.

Many people in Male have two jobs, particularly the young people. There is a system of bonded labour under which people must work for the government in the morning for a meagre wage and then pursue their chosen occupation for the rest of the day to make ends meet.

This system means that many government departments are overstaffed with people who do very little and don't want to be there. When you go to the Atolls Administration for instance, the service can be painfully slow and frustrating by western standards. Patience and politeness are naturally advised, but I must say that the odd, well-timed tantrum doesn't go amiss.

Maldivians generally do not volunteer help and information to visitors. They'll only answer what is asked. If you ask where X is, you will be told X is in Y street; full stop. They will not tell you how to get there or what there is to see there or if it no longer exists. You must ask separate questions to elicit that information.

Since Islam forbids alcohol many Sri Lankans have been brought over to fill key management positions in resorts, creating a situation resented by Maldivians who have to contend with bouts of high unemployment and low wages. Advancement in any form still tends to be determined by who, rather than what, you know, proving that the class system which existed under the sultans still unofficially applies. As an outsider, it's worth keeping this in mind when you want something.

The adult literacy rate is around 86%. In the atolls there are two types of school: the traditional Islamic *maktabs*, and the atoll education centres which offer a broader curriculum. In Male there are medium schools which take students up to the English GCE 'O' Level standard and the Science Education Centre which teaches to 'A' Level. English is taught as a second language. Most official forms and publications are printed in both Dhivehi and English.

The average life expectancy in the Maldives is 52 years; an improvement on the 1977 average which was only 46 years.

CULTURE & SPORT

Sadly, but predictably, western influences are having a greater effect on the Maldives each year. Videos are the rage, pop music blares out of stores and Michael Jackson T-shirts hang on many young shoulders.

The Dhivehi culture is slowly eroding and becoming harder to witness, though you can still catch a glimpse of it at the beginning and end of Ramadan and during other holidays and festivals.

Song & Dance

The *bodu beru* drum music is the best known and most performed traditional music. It is what the tourist resort will put on for a local culture night.

There are dances performed to the bodu beru where the participants begin with a slow, nonchalant swaying and swinging of the arms and end in a frenzied state, with some of the dancers entering a trance-like state. One such dance, the *tara*, finishes with the dancers hitting their heads with spikes until they start to bleed. The *tara* has been banned by the government.

More acceptable is the *bandiya jehun* where young women dance and beat metal pots held under their arms. It is a popular dance on Toddu, to the west of North Male Atoll, and on Mahibadu in nearby Alif (Ari Atoll).

The author of one local tourist guide, when describing the *tharaa* form of folk music, wrote: 'a line of men sit on the ground and beat hand drums (not unlike trampolines) while other men dance between them'. No trampolines accompany the *raivaru* folk song, although they would give some much needed bounce to this 'old type of poetry sung in a dragging tune'!

Most agreeable to western ears are the love songs. You can buy cassettes of these and also bodu beru music for Rf 15 in several Male music stores. Ask to hear the tape by Hassan Fulu.

Sports & Games

With so little open space in the Maldives, it seems quite amazing that soccer and cricket are the national sports.

Soccer is an all-year affair. On every island there is a daily football match among the young men; it's sort of like an afternoon ritual. There's a league competition in Male, played at the National Stadium on Majidi Magu, between teams with names such as 'Renown' and 'Victory'. There is also an annual tournament against teams from Sri Lanka.

Cricket, perhaps the only legacy of the British, is also played at the stadium for a few months, beginning in March. Maldivians keenly follow the fortunes of Sri Lanka, India and the other cricketing countries.

On a more traditional level there is: *mandi*, a game which sounds like an Indonesian shower and looks like primitive lacrosse, in which players with long sticks have to hurl and catch a small stick; and *bai bala*, which is Maldivian tag-wrestling. There are no regular public exhibitions of either game.

You will, however, see men playing *ouvalhugon'di*, a board game with seeds.

Smoking

In the Maldives the cheapest cigarettes you will find are *bidis*, made from imported tobacco rolled in newspaper. Cigarettes can cost up to Rf 5 for packet of 20.

More pleasant to smell, and occasionally taste, is the water-cooled hookah or hubble-bubble. The mixture of tobacco flavoured by honey and coconut gives off a lovely aroma.

RELIGION

Islam is the religion of the Maldives and those who practise it are called Muslims. All Maldivians are Muslims of the Sunni sect, as opposed to the Shi'ite sect. There are no other religions or sects present or permitted in the country.

Islam shares its roots with two of the other major religions, Judaism and

Christianity, and its teachings correspond closely with the Torah, the Old Testament and Gospels. The essence of Islam, however, is the Koran and the Prophet Mohammed.

Adam, Abraham, Noah, Moses and Jesus are all accepted as Muslim prophets, although Jesus is not recognised as the son of God. According to Islam, all of these prophets received the word of Allah (God) but only Mohammed received the complete revelation.

Mohammed was born in Mecca (now in Saudi Arabia) in 570 AD and had his first revelation from Allah in 610. He began to preach against the idolatry that was rampant in the region, particularly in Mecca, and proved to be a powerful and persuasive speaker attracting a devoted following. His teachings appealed to the poorer levels of society and angered the wealthy merchant class.

By 622 life for Mohammed and his followers became so unpleasant that they were forced to migrate to Medina, 300 km to the north. This migration, known as the *Hejira*, marks the start of the Islamic Calendar: 622 AD became year 1 AH.

In 630 AD Mohammed had gained enough followers to return and take Mecca. Within two decades of Mohammed's death most of Arabia had converted to Islam. With seemingly unlimited ambition and zeal the Prophet's followers spread the word, using force where necessary, and the influence of the Islamic state soon extended from the Atlantic to the Indian Ocean.

Islam in the Maldives is fundamental to all aspects of life; there's no getting away from it unless you go to a resort. It is, however, Islam of a more liberal nature than that adhered to in the Arab States; comparable, rather, to the faith practised in India and Indonesia.

Maldivian women, for example, do not have to observe *purdah*, which is the custom of keeping women in seclusion, with clothing that conceals them completely when they go out.

Children are taught the Arabic alphabet and, until their mid teens, attend a *maktab*, one of the traditional Islamic schools where the reading and reciting of the Koran is taught.

There are mosques for the men and for the women. Most are of simple, unadorned design, both inside and out and, apart from the new Islamic Centre in Male, they are not much to look at.

The Five Pillars of Islam

Islam is the Arabic word for submission and underlies the duty of all Muslims to submit themselves to Allah.

Shahada, the profession of faith that 'There is no God but Allah and Mohammed is his prophet', is the first of the Five Pillars of Islam – the tenets that guide Muslims in their daily life.

This first pillar is accomplished through prayer which, in turn, is the second pillar. *Salah* is the call to prayer and Islam decrees that Muslims must face Mecca and pray five times each day.

The third pillar is *zakat*, the act of giving alms to the needy. Some Islamic countries have turned this into an obligatory land tax which goes to help the poor.

All Muslims must fast during the day for the month of *Ramadan*, the ninth month of the Islamic calendar.

The fifth pillar is the *haj* or pilgrimage to Mecca, the holiest place in Islam. It is the duty of every Muslim who is able, to make the *haj* at least once in their life.

Prayer Times

The initial prayer session is in the first hour before sunrise, the second around noon, the third in mid-afternoon about 3.30 pm, the fourth at sunset, and the final session in early evening.

The call to prayer is delivered by the *mudeem* or *muezzin*. In former days, he climbed to the top of the minaret and shouted it out. Now a cassette recording, relayed by loudspeakers on the minaret,

announces the call and the mudeem even appears on TV.

Shops and offices close for 15 minutes after each call. Some people go to the mosque, some kneel where they are and others don't bother.

Ramadan

The fourth pillar of Islam is the fast during the month of Ramadan, which begins at the time of a full moon and ends with the sighting of the new moon. The Ramadan month varies from year to year but is usually sometime between February and April.

During Ramadan Muslims do not eat, drink, smoke or have sex between sunrise and sunset, and working hours are restricted. Exceptions are granted to young children, pregnant or menstruating women and those who are travelling. It is a difficult time for visitors, as cafes are closed during the day and everybody is generally on edge. The evenings, however, are long and lively.

Marriage & Divorce

A Mexican divorce is a long, drawn-out affair compared to a Maldivian divorce.

All the man has to do is to say 'I divorce you', or words to that effect, three times in quick succession; notify the local minister or gazi; and that's the end of the marriage. No formalities or questions asked.

Many couples are married one day and divorced the next. He'll go fishing and that's the last she sees of him, and in many cases, she is truly left carrying the baby. It is not uncommon to find men who have been married more than 20 times and no surprise to learn that the Maldives has the highest rate of divorce in the world. In 1985 there were 2228 marriages and 1928 divorces in Male alone. As a consequence, Maldivians, unlike the Muslims of the Comoros, do not go in for elaborate, expensive weddings.

Men who can afford it are permitted to have more than one wife, but there is little reason to, apart from the status symbol. Gossip is rife, but not promiscuity. Religion, the family and the birth rate make sure of that. Birth control devices are illegal.

Circumcision

A circumcision is a big celebration in the Maldives and worth going to if you can get an invitation. The celebrations for this event seem to make up for the lack of wedding ceremonies and, more to the point, for the pain experienced by the six-year-old child. In fact, the festivities are held to entertain the snipped boy. Often several boys will be done at once and there will be one big carnival to save expense.

The boys lie on their beds, or wooden platforms, each with a sheet suspended over their lower bodies while the merriment continues around them. There is singing, dancing and lots to eat – for the guests; it takes the youngsters three days to get back on their feet.

You'll know when a circumcision party is in progress by the noise and the coloured lights which often decorate the house and yard. Most circumcisions take place during the school holidays.

Local Beliefs

In the islands people still fear *jinnis*, the evil spirits which come from the sea, land and sky. They are blamed for everything that can't be explained by religion or education.

To combat jinnis there are *fandita*, which are the spells and potions provided by the local *hakeem* or medicine man. The hakeem is often called upon when illness strikes, if a woman fails to conceive, or if the fishing catch is poor.

The hakeem might cast a curing spell by writing phrases from the Koran on strips of paper and sticking or tying them to the patient. Another method is to write the sayings in ink on a plate, fill the plate with water to dissolve the ink and make the patient drink the potion.

Other concoctions include *isitri*, a love potion used in matchmaking, and its antidote *varitoli* which is used to break up marriages. Judging by the divorce statistics it isn't really needed; or perhaps it's overused.

HOLIDAYS & FESTIVALS

Most holidays are based on the Islamic lunar calendar and the dates vary from year to year.

Ramadan
Known as *rorda mas* in the Maldives, this is the Islamic month of fasting. Ramadan is the most important religious event and will occur from late March to late April in 1990; from mid-March to mid-April in 1991; the first week of March to the first week of April in 1992; and late February to late March in 1993.

Kuda Id
This occurs at the end of Ramadan, with the sighting of the new moon, and is celebrated with a feast.

Prophet's Birthday
The birthday of the Prophet Mohammed is celebrated with three days of eating and merriment. The dates are: 1-2 October 1990; 20-21 September 1991; 9-10 September 1992; and 29-30 August 1993.

Huravee Day
The day the Malabars of India were kicked out by Sultan Hassan Izzuddeen after their brief occupation in 1752.

Martyr's Day
Commemorates the death of Sultan Ali VI at the hands of the Portuguese in 1558.

Fixed holiday dates are:

New Year's Day
1 January

National Day
A major event celebrating the day Mohammed Thakurufaan and his men overthrew the Portuguese on Male in 1578.

Independence Day
26 July – the day the British protectorate ended.

Republic Day
11 November – commemorates the second (current) republic, founded in 1968.

Fisheries Day
10 December

LANGUAGE

The language of the Maldives is Dhivehi. It is closely related to an ancient form of Sinhala, a Sri Lankan language, but also contains some Arabic and Hindi words.

Dhivehi has its own script, Tana, which was introduced by the great Maldivian hero Thakurufaan after he tossed out the Portuguese in the 16th century. Tana looks like shorthand and is read from right to left (their front page is our back page). There are 24 letters in the alphabet.

The first thing you should know about the language is that Maldives is pronounced *mawl-divs* – as in 'gives' not 'dives'.

On most islands you'd be very lucky to find anyone who speaks anything other than Dhivehi, although you can get around Male and Hitadu easily enough with just English. Hitadu is the capital of Seenu, the southernmost atoll, where the British employed most of the islanders on the air base for 20 years.

Obviously it would be nice to have a few phrases up your sleeve for impressing or entertaining Maldivians. But whenever I tried to rattle off a query or comment in the local tongue I was met with blank stares. It appears that knowing the words or phrases is only half the battle. It's the rhythm and pronunciation that trips you up. Rather than being honoured and delighted that I had attempted their language, people asked 'Why don't you speak English? It'll be easier for all of us.'

The romanised transliteration of the language is a potpourri of phonetic approximations, and words can be spelt in a variety of ways. This is most obvious if you study Maldivian place names. For example: Majidi Magu is also spelt Majeedhee and Majeedee; Sosun Ge could be Soasan Ge; Hitadu becomes Hithadhu and Hithadhoo; and Fuamulak can be Fua Mulaku or, thanks to one 19th century mariner, Phoowa Moloku.

To add to the confusion several islands have the same name (there are six called Viligili!), and there are both traditional *and* administrative names for each of the 19 atolls. On top of all this, dialects vary throughout the country.

The government is party to these variations. There seems to be no officially correct, or even consistent, spelling of Dhivehi words in their English literature. For the sake of uniformity in this book I have tried to keep to the most basic spelling and have not added vowels or consonants if they do not radically affect the pronunciation.

I could not find a good phrasebook for visitors. Either no-one has tried to produce one or the project's been dumped. Here are a few examples which may prove useless:

Maldivian National Anthem

Greetings & Civilities

hello/farewell	*a-salam alekum*
peace	*salam*
How are you?	*haalu kihine?*
Very well (reply)	*vara gada*
See you later	*fahung badaluvang*
fine, good, great	*barabah*
OK	*enge*
thank you	*shukuria*

Some Useful Words

I, me	*Aharen, ma*

you, she, he	*kale, mina, ena*
name	*nang, nama*
yes	*aa*
no	*noo*
expensive	*agu bodu*
very expensive	*vara agu bodu*
cheap	*agu heyo*
enough	*heo*
now	*mihaaru*
little (for people, places)	*kuda*
mosquito	*madiri*
mosquito net	*madiri ge*
toilet	*gifili*
inside	*etere*
outside	*berufarai*
water (rain, well)	*vaare feng, valu feng*

Some Useful Verbs

swim	*fatani*
eat	*kani*
walk	*hingani*
sleep	*nidani*
sail	*duvani*
go	*dani*
stay	*hunani*
dance	*nashani*
wash	*donani*

Some Useful Phrases

How much is this?	*mi kihavaraka?*
What is that?	*e korche?*
What did you say?	*kike?*
I'm going	*Aharen dani*
Where are you going?	*kong taka dani?*
How much is the fare?	*fi kihavare?*

People

friend	*ratehi*
father, mother	*bapa, mama*
atoll chief	*atolu verin*
island chief	*kateeb*
VIP, upper class person	*befalu*
white person (tourist or expat)	*don miha*

community religious leader	*gazi*
prayer caller	*mudeem*
fisherman	*mas veri*
toddy man	*ra veri*
evil spirit	*jinni*

Places

atoll	*atolu*
island	*fushi*
sandbank	*finolhu*
reef or lagoon	*faru*
street	*magu*
lane or small street	*golhi* or *higun*
mosque	*miski*
house	*ge*

Time & Days

Monday	*Horma*
Tuesday	*Angaara*
Wednesday	*Buda*
Thursday	*Brassfati*
Friday	*Hukuru*
Saturday	*Honihiu*
Sunday	*Aadita*
day	*duvas*
week	*hafta*
month	*mas*
year	*aharu*
tomorrow	*madamma*
today	*miadu*
yesterday	*iye*
tonight	*mire*

Numbers

1	*eke*
2	*de*
3	*tine*
4	*hatare*
5	*fahe*
6	*haie*
7	*hate*
8	*ashe*
9	*nue*
10	*diha*
11	*egaara*
12	*baara*
13	*tera*
14	*saada*

15	fanara	40	saalis
16	sorla	50	fansaas
17	satara	60	fasdolaas
18	ashara	70	hai-diha
19	onavihi	80	a-diha
20	vihi	90	nua-diha
30	tiris	100	sateka

VISAS

Visas are not required by any nationality except Sri Lankans. Israeli passport holders should make advance enquiries to determine if they will be permitted entry or not.

You get a one-month visitor's permit (no fee) on arrival unless you're Indian, Pakistani, Bangladeshi or Italian, in which case you get a 90 day permit. It is difficult to extend this permit (see the following section) unless you continue to stay on resorts and have sufficient funds.

If you want to apply for an extension go to the Department of Immigration (tel 323913) in the Huravee Building next to the police station in Male. Extensions are granted for up to an additional three months at Rf 300 for each extension.

On arrival visitors who are not on a package tour are supposed to show they have at least US$10 for each day of their stay and an outgoing ticket.

Work Visas

Work permits are issued but they are mainly for tourism-related employment.

PERMITS

A few years ago a group of Italian tourists invaded an island, threw off their clothes and tried to convert the fishing community back to sunworshipping. Ever since then all inhabited islands have been declared off-limits to travellers.

The days of casual island-hopping are over as the government resolves to keep Muslim Maldivian society separate from and untainted by western ways. You now must apply to the Ministry of Atolls Administration, next to Air Maldives in the Fashanaa Building on Marine Drive in Male, for a permit to visit any island, other than a resort, which is inhabited.

This permission is difficult to get; you must come up with a batch of credentials and a good reason other than for the 'joy and adventure of travel and discovery'.

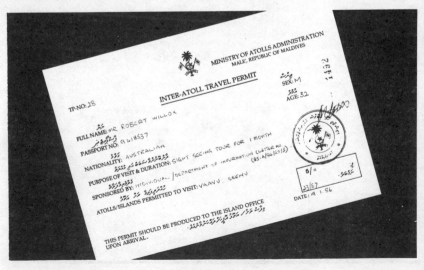

For example, visits for research purposes related to anthropology, health, religion, flora, fauna, crafts, photography, journalism, etc stand a good chance of approval providing they are supported with references from universities, associations, companies, journals and so forth.

It also may be worth approaching your country's consular representative or writing to the relevant government departments in Male for their backing. The more official-looking names and paperwork you have, the better.

Another way is to have a 'very good friend' on the island who will be prepared to vouch for you, feed and accommodate you. This support must be given in writing, preferably with an OK from the *kateeb* (island chief), and submitted with your application. (The letter must come from the island not from Male.)

As it is unlikely you already have contacts in the Maldives, you will need to make friends quickly on arrival in Male. Guest house managers/owners and souvenir salespeople are good starting points. Most Male residents will have friends or family on various atolls, which of course will determine your choice of island.

Getting a letter of support-cum-invitation back from the island, however, could take up to two weeks depending on how isolated it is from Male.

The Atolls Administration itself is slow and discouraging so perseverance and patience are necessary. If you succeed, you pay Rf 5 for the permit which will specify which atolls or islands you can visit. Try and get an atoll approval which will give you authority to visit any island within it. Permits are issued only before 11 am.

As soon as you land on an island you must go to the island office to present the permit. Don't land without one as island and atoll chiefs are fearful of breaking these rules, so they will enforce them.

Outside of Male and the resorts the only atoll you may sneak a visit to without a permit is Seenu (traditionally called Addu Atoll). (Strictly speaking you should have permission from the Addu Development Authority as well as a permit.) Getting there, however, is not that simple. You must fly to Gan and stay at the 'Holiday Village' – the former RAF officers' and sergeants' mess! From there you are linked by causeways to Hitadu, Maradu and Feydu.

Most resorts run day trips to inhabited and uninhabited islands, including Male if they're close enough, mostly to buy and sell souvenirs.

CUSTOMS

Male International Airport is on Hulhule Island, two km across the water from the capital. Customs, immigration and health checks are relatively perfunctory if you are on the way to a resort with all the other passengers; or if it looks like you are.

Because the Maldives is an Islamic nation, no alcohol or pornography can be brought into the country. You will probably get your duty-free bottle of Scotch back when you leave, but I don't know if they'll return a copy of *Playboy*.

You will be asked on the immigration form where you are staying. If you have not booked a place, put down the the name of any resort, otherwise the immigration officials will make you arrange accommodation somewhere before they let you leave the airport.

MONEY

The unit of currency is the rufiya (Rf), which is divided into 100 larees. Notes come in denominations of 100, 50, 20, 10, five and two rufiya. There is a Rf 1 coin, and laree pieces are in denominations of 50, 25, 10, five, two and one.

Bring your money in US dollars because that currency carries the most weight in the Maldives. Visitors must pay accommodation and most travel expenses with the greenback. Guest houses will take travellers' cheques.

There are no currency restrictions when

you change money into rufiya but you are only allowed to re-convert 10% of that amount on departure, and only then if you have the original bill of exchange. So don't get caught with too much rufiya at the end of your visit.

US$ 1 =	Rf	9.5
A$ 1 =	Rf	6.5
UK£1 =	Rf	15.5
C$ 1 =	Rf	7
DM 1 =	Rf	5
Fr 1 =	Rf	1.5
Y 1 =	Rf	0.06

The exchange rate is published daily in the *Haveeru* newspaper in Dhivehi script.

Banks
The six banks in Male are clustered at the harbour end of Chandani Magu and along Marine Drive (East). They are open Sunday to Thursday, from 9 am to 1 pm, and on Saturday from 9 to 11 am. They are closed on Fridays.

Some banks may tell you that reconversion of currency can only be done at the airport bank when you leave. This is not the case. If you encounter any problems, you can threaten to go to the Monetary Authority (behind the post office in Male) to check or complain.

Some banks have been known not to accept travellers' cheques in currencies other than the US dollar or UK pound because of 'transfer problems with correspondents'. In other words, they have had difficulty cashing them. There were no such problems with the Habib Bank in Male, which I also found to be the most efficient.

Black Market
Until mid-1987, there was an active black market in currency. There were plenty of unofficial moneychangers in Male and little danger from authorities. The black market no longer exists, however, as the government has set more realistic rates for buying and selling rufiya.

Credit Cards
Major credit cards are accepted. The American Express representative is Treasure Island Enterprises (tel 323745) on Marine Drive.

Bargaining
Bargaining is limited to the tourist shops in and around the Singapore Bazaar in Male and at island village stalls where prices are not fixed. Because most tourists come on brief one-off shopping excursions from the resorts, some traders will charge what they feel they can get away with,

knowing there is little chance an unhappy customer will return.

TIPPING
There is a 10% service charge in many resorts, but not in the restaurants and cafes of Male. Airport porters obviously expect a reasonable tip; Rf 10 or US$1 is usual.

TOURIST INFORMATION
There is a Department of Tourism information office, between the Foreign Affairs ministry offices and Air Lanka on Marine Drive in Male, which offers minimal tourist literature and advice. They'll give you a free map of Male Island and Atoll and neighbouring Alif Atoll with a list of resorts. You can also buy other colourful maps, books, postcards and souvenirs.

For more specific enquiries, go to the Department of Tourism head office (tel 323224/8) in the Ghaazee Building opposite the police station.

The adjacent Huravee Building houses the Department of Information & Broadcasting (tel 323837) which is responsible for Maldives TV and radio. They issue a fortnightly news sheet in English and will assist with any legitimate research.

Overseas Reps
For advance information on the country contact:

Austria
Gerald Wiedler, Peter Jordan Strasse 21-250, 1190 Wien (tel 343438)
Japan
Tsuyoshi Fumizono, 712, 5-10 1-Chome, Kamimeguro, Meguro-ku, Tokyo (tel 03 7113511)
Sri Lanka
Maldivian High Commission, 25 Melbourne Ave, Colombo 4 (tel 586762)
Sweden
Stephen Ericson, Gamla Brogatan 32, S-11120, Stockholm (tel 46(8)-247550)

Switzerland
Marc Odermatt, Gerechtigkeitsgasse 23, 8002 Zurich (tel 01-2029785)
UK
Maldives Department of Tourism, Glebe House, Welder's Lane, Chalfont St Peter, Bucks (tel 02407-3129)
West Germany
Maldivian Consul, Immanuel Kant Strasse 16, D-6380 Bad Homburg (tel 6902624)

Foreign Consuls
The diplomatic corps in the Maldives is not very large.

Denmark/Sweden
Abdulla Saeed, Cyprea, 25 Marine Drive (tel 322451)
France
Mohamed Ismail Manik, 27 Chandani Magu (tel 323760)
India
High Commission, Orchid Magu (tel 323015). They do not issue tourist visas for India. You have to go to Colombo to get one.
USA
Rasheeda Mohamed Didi, Violet Magu (off Sosun Magu) (tel 322581)
West Germany
Farouk Ismail, 10 Fardidi Magu (tel 322669)

There is no British or Australian representation. If you lose your passport, you will have to get an identity certificate from the Department of Immigration to get you to Colombo or Singapore. Australian, US, UK, Canadian and most Western European nationals do not need a visa to enter Sri Lanka. Sri Lanka does have a diplomatic mission in the Maldives, as do Pakistan and Bangladesh. Libya and the PLO are also said to have official representatives in Male.

Voluntary Organisations
The lack of diplomatic representation is compensated for by a multinational community of voluntary workers.

Voluntary organisations are another source of information and prospective help in an emergency. These organisations are led by the 25-strong brigade of the British Voluntary Service Overseas (VSO). The VSO offices (tel 323167) are at Nooraanee Aage on Orchid Magu. Ask for the Field Director.

The VSO, whose volunteers work in nursing, planning, teaching and other roles, is supplemented by Australian volunteers. The Japanese take charge of dentistry and sports. The Danish and Americans are involved in health, while Norway and the US run the Save the Children missions.

There are also the United Nations agencies: UNDP, UNICEF and UNESCO. The UN Development Programme (UNDP) predominates, providing aid to the agriculture, fishing and craft industries. The office (tel 324501/2/3) is in Kulidoshi Magu.

The volunteers, together with other expatriates, can be contacted informally at the bars of the Alia and Nasandhura hotels between 6 and 11 pm.

GENERAL INFORMATION
Post
The post office is on the corner of Chandani Magu and Marine Drive in Male. The hours are officially listed as 7.30 am to 1.30 pm and 3 to 5 pm, but the office is actually open daily, except Friday, from 7.30 am to 12.45 pm and from 4 to 5.50 pm. (These hours are strange but precise.)

To send a postcard anywhere overseas costs Rf 2 and a standard airmail letter costs Rf 3. Complications start with parcel post and customs formalities. There is a poste restante service.

Telephones
A new national telephone service started in 1988. All Male numbers are prefixed with 32 and numbers on other islands (the resorts) with 34.

Public telephones are few and far between, but shopkeepers will let you use their phone for Rf 2 a local call. You can also call overseas from any private phone

which has been registered for international calls, either through the international operator in Male (tel 190) or by direct dialling. Alternatively you can go to Cable & Wireless on Medu Ziyaaraiy Magu, near the intersection with Chandani Magu.

Before the new exchange opened, the charges were Rf 72 for the first three minutes to Europe, Australia or the USA, and Rf 24 for each additional minute. A person to person call was Rf 96 for the first three minutes. But these rates could be eventually reduced by as much as 50% with International Direct Dialling.

Most resorts can be contacted directly by private phone. The atoll offices are linked to Male and to each other by radiotelephone and between islands by CB radio. To contact someone on an island through their atoll office, you have to book the call a day in advance at the Department of P&T in Male at a cost of Rf 5 for three minutes. Some private phones are registered for inter-atoll communications.

The new Japanese-built Post & Telecommunications is on Husnuheenaa

Magu, just down from the Olympus Cinema in Male.

Electricity
Electricity is 220-240 volts, 50 cycles AC and plug sockets vary, so you'd better bring an adapter if you've got a lot to switch on. In Male the electricity supply is reasonably reliable.

There is no national grid and power is supplied by generators. The fuel to power those generators is one of the resorts' major expenses. About half the islands in the country have generators and power is restricted, in most cases, to the evening between 6 and 11 pm. The other islands rely on kerosene and candles. For that reason, a torch could come in very useful.

Time
The Maldives is five hours ahead of GMT. They are in the same time zone as Pakistan, half an hour behind India and Sri Lanka, and three hours behind Singapore.

Business Hours
Government offices are open every day, except Friday, from 7.30 am to 1.30 pm. During the month of Ramadan hours are 9 am to 1 pm.

Shop hours vary. In Male the shops at the bottom of Chandani Magu open earlier and those on Majidi Magu close later but in general they all open between 7 and 8 am and close between 9 and 11 pm every day, including Friday. These hours are interrupted by prayer calls when doors close for about 15 minutes. The streets are quietest around the time of the last two prayer calls, between about 6 and 8 pm, although lunchtime from 1.30 to 3 pm is also quiet.

Weights & Measures
We have used metric measurement in this book. For those unaccustomed to this system there is a metric/imperial conversion chart at the end of the book.

Laundry
If you want shirts, dresses or trousers washed, there are two or three laundries on Majidi Magu in Male which charge Rf 1.50 an item.

MEDIA
Newspapers & Magazines
The Maldives has one daily paper, the *Haveeru*, which has a circulation of 1000 and is available only in Male. It costs Rf 1 and usually has around eight pages, one of which is devoted to news in English. The cinema advertisements are also in English and you should be able to understand the prayer times. Horoscopes and exchange rates are in Dhivehi.

Until mid-1987 the paper was written by hand, then copied and printed. There was only one typewriter with Dhivehi characters in the whole country and it was used by the president's office. New 'nationalised' typewriters are now apparently being used.

Every fortnight there is an eight page, Rf 2 edition of the *Spectrum* newspaper, which deals with sport and feature articles, and a *News Bulletin* from the Department of Information. Both are in English.

Hindi film papers and magazines are popular, and copies of *Time* and *Newsweek* are available from Novelty and Asrafee bookshops and on resorts.

Radio & Television

The Voice of Maldives radio is broadcast to the whole country for 11 hours each day. The news, in English, is read at 6 pm for 10 minutes, following a half-hour pop music show from Radio Australia. A new transmitter and studios were built with Australian aid.

TV Maldives, which started in 1978, broadcasts for up to five hours a day during the week, with an extended service on weekends. It only transmits within a 30 km radius of Male. There is a daily 20-minute news bulletin in English at 9 pm.

HEALTH

Although it is continually being upgraded, the Maldives health service is very limited and relies heavily on volunteer doctors, nurses and dentists from overseas.

The main Central Hospital is on Sosun Magu in Male. There are also hospitals on Ugufaaru, the capital of Raa; Kuludufushi in Haa Dhaal; Hitadu on Seenu; and, the latest, in Muli on Meemu. They all suffer from inadequate supplies of drugs and staff. The other atoll capitals each have a health centre staffed by a health worker who has had basic training.

There's a volunteer Japanese dentist in Male who does cheap, professional dental work. Fees for a medical consultation and treatment are not high.

The atoll hospitals and health centres can treat minor illnesses, while Male's Central Hospital, which has Russian doctors, can deal with routine operations but post-operative treatment is not up to western standards.

This basically means that getting seriously ill in the Maldives is not recommended. Cases that require specialist operations must be evacuated to Colombo or back home. Check your insurance policy to see if you are covered for the worst. You'll come across several Maldivians saving up to go to Colombo or New Delhi for treatment.

The Flying Swiss Ambulance service, supplemented by the Inter-Atoll Air company's flying boat, takes care of emergency cases on the resorts. To insure against high medical evacuation fees, should you have the misfortune to get that sick, you can join the Flying Swiss Ambulance Maldives (FSAM) before you leave home. Just write to the organisation's headquarters: Flying Swiss Ambulance, Postfach 259, FL-9495 Triesen, Switzerland. The telephone number is 075 26666. Fees are US$19 for adults and US$32 for a family. The FSAM office (tel 324500) in Male is on Marine Drive.

Remember, if you're planning to go diving, to make sure that your travel insurance covers you for diving.

Vaccinations

The health regulations require that you are immunised against cholera and yellow fever if arriving from an infected area. Vaccinations against tetanus and hepatitis are advisable if you are travelling further afield than Male or one of the resorts.

If you have come from Sri Lanka or India, looking the worse for wear, you could find yourself having a blood test, vaccination and one week quarantine in Male before you get the OK by the immigration department to visit the country. This is unlikely, however, since officials tend to concentrate on Indian and Sri Lankan visitors, many of whom arrive with insufficient funds.

Health Precautions

Drink only rainwater or water which has been boiled or sterilised. Never take a chance on the water served in Male cafes or water from village wells. It's a good idea to include iodine solution or water purification tablets in your first aid kit.

Bring with you from home any medication you think you will need. There are three pharmacies in Male, all around Majidi and Sosun magus near the hospital.

Common Ailments

Malaria has officially been wiped out in the Maldives. There are, however, still cases of the disease even if the government prefers to register them as something else. So make sure you're on a course of anti-malarials (see the general Health section).

The strength of the mosquito squadrons varies from island to island. They are not a problem in Male and the resorts are generally mosquito-free around living areas. To combat them use coils if you can put up with the smell, fast ceiling fans if you can put up with the draught, or air-con if you can put up with the money.

As in India and Sri Lanka, diarrhoea and stomach ailments are common in the Maldives. The biggest danger though is most likely to come from infected cuts. If you plan a lot of diving or snorkelling, there is an increased risk from coral cuts. Refer to the Health section in the general Facts for the Visitor chapter.

DANGERS & ANNOYANCES
Security
The Maldives police consist of a civilian and a military force. The latter are involved in guarding the president, airport and other sensitive subjects and although they sport the usual olive green fatigues, berets and Boer War surplus rifles, they maintain a low profile and do not disturb visitors.

The civilian police are relatively efficient but hard to identify. The only uniform apparent on many is a light blue shirt. Unless there's a chevron or two on the sleeve, you can't tell if it's a policeman.

There is something not quite right about Maldivian justice. While you can applaud the fact that it is not as barbaric (to western senses) as that of some Arab countries, you can criticise it for not being strict enough.

In the Maldives instead of chopping off hands for theft or dishing out 50 lashes for drinking whisky, they banish criminals and political prisoners to an island other than their home island.

Some people argue that this is a devastating punishment since the offenders are taken away from their families and friends for years at a time. But the contrary seems to be more often the case. Several former prisoners, banished during various political upheavals, have told me they thoroughly enjoyed their exile. They were looked after by villagers who gave them special treatment and they didn't have to work hard. One man said it was the happiest time of his life.

On an island in the extreme north of North Male Atoll lives a German traveller who was banished to the island in 1976 after being convicted of the murder of his girlfriend. He is now married to a local girl, has two children and has resisted all attempts by the West German government and consul to have him extradited to serve his sentence at home.

Theft
Crimes of violence and theft are not a pressing problem in the Maldives. There are occasional thefts from resort rooms and on island village tours, but tourists generally are safe.

Each year 2000 criminals are convicted, of whom more than half are banished. A young man I met, called Hassan Hussain, was one of those banished.

I was a guest of the kateeb (island chief) on Felidu, the capital of Felidu Atoll. Hassan was his son-in-law. One day I joined the other young men of the village for the daily soccer match. I had to keep goals as I had no suitable shoes to run about in. Hassan was the only other person playing in bare feet. He was on my side and we had a laugh together about it.

The next morning I awoke to find the bag containing my wallet, research and camera equipment gone. Someone had sneaked into my bedroom and snatched it. It could have been any one of the 300 villagers. A search was called anyway.

Hassan had gone fishing early in the morning. When I found out he had a record for theft, he became the prime suspect. The atoll office radio-telephoned the police with the registration number of the fishing dhoni to see if it had arrived in Male to sell the catch. Helped by nearby resorts and friendly island officials, I returned to the capital immediately.

When I arrived, I learnt that Hassan had been questioned, released and re-arrested. Police had met the boat and searched it. Hassan was clean. Then he made the mistake of going to change money with a mutual friend – the same friend who had arranged for me to visit Felidu and had been told of the theft. The amount of US dollars Hassan tried to change was the same amount of money I had reported missing. The police were informed and Hassan was brought in for tougher questioning.

Hassan confessed and told police he had buried my bag by the shore in Felidu and gone to Male with the money. Back on the island they recovered my bag and sent the soggy contents to me on the next fishing dhoni. Only the camera was ruined – salt water had seeped into the works.

I was told Hassan would be banished again, probably for three years. I felt sorry for his wife, but knowing what I did about divorces and good times in exile, I couldn't sympathise with Hassan's supposed plight. Still, I wouldn't have wanted them to cut his hands off.

FILM & PHOTOGRAPHY

If the Maldives is a paradise for anyone other than divers, it's photographers. While in reality the islands may not be paradise to live on, they certainly are to look at and, together with the Seychelles, are a popular location for advertising shoots.

The photographer given the most exposure for his shots of Maldivian islands is probably Michael Friedel of Munich. You'll see his photos in brochures and on postcards. Also keep an eye out for the underwater photography of Japan's Katsutoshi-Ito.

Colour film is available in several shops, but it is often safer and cheaper to go to the photographic studios. Black & white film and video film are also available. Resorts which specialise in diving usually have underwater photographic equipment to rent.

Fototeknik, opposite Olympus Cinema on Majidi Magu, is the Kodak agent. Kodak Gold 100 ASA 36/24 exposure film costs Rf 40/32. Kodachrome 64 ASA 36

exposure slide film costs Rf 122, but it is not developed in the country. Colour developing and printing generally costs Rf 137/98 for 36/24 exposures. A print album is an extra Rf 10.

Centofoto and Fotogenic are also on Majidi Magu. The latter charges Rf 2.50 per print and a Rf 20 developing fee, which works out cheaper than Fototeknik. They all do repairs.

Remember: don't take pictures of people while they're praying; and don't photograph the Muleeaage (president's office) which is on Meduziyaraiy Magu opposite the Hukuru Miski (mosque), or the Theemuge, (president's residence) which is on Orchid Magu, or the airport, or any police barracks. Don't despair if the skies are cloudy as this often results in better effects and contrasts.

ACCOMMODATION
Hotels & Guest Houses
Apart from the resort islands, the only official accommodation is provided by two hotels, a holiday village in Gan and 36 guest houses on Male.

Unless you want air-con or have an expense account there is no reason to stay at the hotels. Some resort tourists, however, may find themselves at a hotel on the first night if bad weather prevents the boat transfer to the resort. The rooms are basic and soulless. You'll find several guest houses that are just as good for a third of the price.

All accommodation must be paid for in US dollars. The rates quoted should include the US$6 per night government bed tax, but double-check. The prices are for a bed only, not a room. Unless you enquire first, you could end up sharing a room with strangers. Some of the better guest houses have special double rates.

The government does little to promote guest houses. In 1983 there were more than 100 guest houses in Male, but since the Indians stopped visiting for duty-free sprees, more than half have closed. Others have been hit for not declaring bed tax, while some suffered when inter-island travel was restricted which also curtailed their sideline travel services. Finally, in 1987 when the black market for the US dollar ended, the guest houses increased their rates considerably.

Still, there is a large choice and conditions range from overcrowded hovels to spacious, clean units. Your biggest problem will be pronouncing some of the names.

Check to see that rooms have a ceiling fan; it makes all the difference in the cramped and stuffy rooms at the bottom end of the market. Guest houses offer only cold water showers. Bring a sleeping sheet; it will prove more comfortable in some places and safer in others.

See the Male chapter for more information on guest houses and hotels, and the Atoll to Atoll chapter for details on resort accommodation.

Island Villages

If you are fortunate enough to stay in an island village, you will be housed where there is room, and not necessarily with your 'friend'. In many cases, particularly on the smaller islands, where you stay will depend on the kateeb (island chief), and it may well be at his home.

Protocol As a matter of protocol, guests should introduce themselves to the kateeb upon arrival or shortly after. If the island is the atoll capital, guests should also introduce themselves to the atoll chief. The other person to make yourself known to is the gazi (champion of the faith), the island's religious leader and judge.

It is always best to dress as smartly as possible when meeting officials. In some ways it helps to justify the respect that will be shown to you at the outset. Wear a shirt rather than a T-shirt, shoes not thongs, and long trousers or a skirt instead of shorts or a sarong. Don't worry about this too much if you arrive by fishing dhoni after spending eight hours at sea. It just helps, that's all.

Homes On the main islands, official visitors are usually put up in the atoll chief's house. These are modern but basic abodes built out of concrete rather than coral. Informal guests will be offered a room with a family.

The average home and surrounding low walls are made from coral stone and mortar. Wooden beams support a palm-thatched or corrugated iron roof. Beds are nothing out of the ordinary, and the mattresses and pillows are filled with coconut matting.

Hanging by rope from the beams or trees are the *undorlis*, which are swinging wooden platforms also known as bed-boats. The undorli is a combination lounge suite and hammock and takes the place of both in Maldivian homes. A variation is the *joli*, made from rope and wood, which is like sitting in a string shopping bag. Often you'll find a three or four seater joli outside the front or back door.

Toilet Less relaxing for western guests is the *gifili* – the bathroom and toilet. In most cases, the toilet is a hole in the ground surrounded by shrubs or a thatched fence. Some places have a manufactured Asian-style drained latrine.

On some islands the beach is still used as a toilet, even though the government is trying to discourage the habit. One part of the beach is reserved for women and another part, some distance away, for men. It is not used until after dusk. The sea is supposed to wash the beach clean by the next morning, but I'd check before snorkelling.

Washing is done around the well, not in it. Water for showering or cleaning is drawn by a large tin can on the end of a long pole. Some homes have a well out front, comparable to the kitchen sink, and another out the back for bathing only.

Other Information Several islands have a generator, but the use of electricity is generally restricted to between 6 and 11 pm, and only used for radios and lights. Apart from this, lighting is provided by candles and hurricane lanterns.

All meals will be provided by your host but to begin with, you may be expected to dine separately from the family. This could be because they think you would prefer to, maybe for religious reasons, or it might simply signify special treatment along with a special menu. Don't worry about it. One more thing, don't drink the water unless you are sure it is rainwater. Never drink well water.

Payment is completely negotiable but you should pay between US$5 and US$10 a day for meals and accommodation, or the equivalent in rufiya at the end of your stay.

FOOD

One of the biggest surprises about the Maldives is the scarcity of luscious fruits and vegetables. It spoils the paradise image, but is perfectly understandable as there's just not the room or soil depth on the tiny coral atolls to produce anything much at all. Only the coconut thrives; most of the rest is imported.

The quality of meals at the resorts is a topic of regular complaint by jetsetting tourists who expect a lot better for their money. Eating tinned fruit salad for a romantic island dinner dessert is tantamount to having frozen fish fingers at an Eskimo feast. To compensate, the resort operators try to cater according to nationality. The Italian resorts, for instance, import lots of pasta.

Fish and rice are the staple foods of the Maldivian people; meat and chicken are saved for special occasions. Their diet in general is poor which probably contributes to their short life expectancy.

If you're going to eat local food, prepare your pallet for fish curry, fish soup, and variations thereof. There is usually not much choice in what you eat, but here is a list of dishes found in the Maldives.

Fish

mas	fish; usually refers to skipjack tuna or bonito
valo mas	smoked fish
teluli mas	fried fish
mas huni & hana kuri mas	dried, tinned, fried or cold fish mixed with onion, chilli or spices
mas riha	fish curry
kandukukulhu	a special tuna curry
garudia	the staple diet of fish soup, often taken with rice, lime, and chilli
rihakuru	garudia boiled down to a salty sauce or paste

Fruit

kurumba	a young or new coconut; applied to any coconut
donkeo	little bananas
bambukeyo	breadfruit
bambukeyo hiti	breadfruit used in curries
bambukeyo bondibai	breadfruit used in desserts
don ambu	mango (green mangoes boiled with sugar are delicious)
falor	papaya or paw paw

Miscellaneous

bai	rice

roshi	pancake bread; eaten with soups and curries
modunu	a simple salad
aluvi	potato
paan	bread
bis	egg
kiru	milk
hakuru	sugar
sa	tea; always white and sweet unless you ask otherwise

Hedhikaa is the selection of sweets and savouries, including *gulas, kuli boakiba, bondi bai, kastad* and *foni boakiba*, that is placed on the tables in Male cafes.

gulas	fish ball; deep fried in flour and rice batter
kuli boakiba	spicy fish cake
bondi bai	rice pudding; sometimes with currants
kastad	sweet custard
foni boakiba	gelatin cakes and puddings

The Maldivian equivalent of the after-dinner mint is the *arecanut*. It is chewed by one and all after any meal or snack. The little oval nuts, from the areca palm, are sliced into thin sections and chewed with betel leaf, cloves and lime (from limestone). Unlike betel nut, it doesn't give you red-rotten teeth but it's still an acquired taste.

DRINKS

There is a reasonable selection of imported foods, alcohol and soft drinks in Male.

Raa is the name for toddy tapped from the crown of the palm trunk at the point where the coconuts grow. Every village has its toddy man or *raa veri*. The *raa* is sweet and delicious if you can get over the pungent smell. Drink it immediately after it is tapped from the tree or leave it to become more alcoholic as the sugar ferments.

BOOKS & BOOKSHOPS

If you plan to do a lot of reading – and often there is little else to do – just take a couple of your own books because you'll probably be able to swap them later with other travellers.

The following is a selection of books which should provide some background on the Maldives.

History

The historian of the Maldives is H C P Bell, a former British commissioner in the Ceylon Civil Service who first visited the islands in 1879 courtesy of a shipwreck.

He returned twice, in 1920 and 1922, to lead archaeological expeditions and published several accounts including *A Description of the Maldive Islands* for the *Journal of the Royal Asiatic Society* (Ceylon Branch, Colombo, 1925),

In 1940, three years after his death, the Ceylon Government Press published his main work *The Maldive Islands: Monograph on the History, Archaeology & Epigraphy*. Original copies of the book are rare, however there are copies in the two Male libraries. The National Centre for Linguistic & Historical Research of the Maldives, based at the National Library, is reprinting the book.

Much of Bell's research on pre-Muslim civilisation has been supported, challenged and expanded by Kon-Tiki explorer Thor Heyerdahl in *The Maldive Mystery* (George Allen & Unwin, London, 1986).

Heyerdahl spent several months during 1982-83 digging around the southern atolls. With the apparent blessing of the Maldives government, he unearthed evidence of early Buddhist, Hindu and sun-worshipping prehistoric societies, each succeeding the other before the arrival of Islam in the 12th century.

Heyerdahl's discoveries are exhibited at the National Museum in Sultan Park. His theories on early navigators and traders have not exactly been embraced by Maldivian authorities, who seem to have a 'we don't really wish to know that' attitude.

For history of the Muslim period, look at Ibn Battuta's *Travels in Asia & Africa 1325-54*, reprinted in paperback by Routledge Kegan Paul in 1983. Ibn Battuta was a great Moorish globetrotter.

Another historical text is *The Story of Mohamed Thakurufaan* by Hussain Salahuddeen (1986) which tells of the Maldives' greatest hero who liberated the people from the Portuguese. It is available in Male from Novelty Bookshop.

General

A well-respected work is *People of the Maldive Islands* by American anthropologist Dr Clarence Maloney (Orient Longman, New Delhi, 1980). Covering past and present, this is the best general reference on the country and is not too academic. Unfortunately, it is not readily available.

More accessible, much cheaper and just as readable is *The Fascinating Maldives* by Mohamed Farook (Novelty Printers, Male, 1985). It sells for Rf 12 at the Novelty Bookshop. Farook, naturally, presents a favourable image of Maldivian society, but it's an honest account.

Maldives: A Nation Of Islands, published by the Department of Tourism in 1983, has plenty of colour plates, though the text goes in for a lot of back-patting and hailing of national achievements. It makes an attractive gift and you can buy it at any souvenir or resort store for about Rf 60.

As well as the explorers, seafarers and several shipwreck victims of days gone by, the odd modern adventurer or two has also bumped into the Maldives. Author and sailor Alan Villiers tells of his brigantine forays in *Give Me a Ship to Sail* (Hodder & Stoughton, London, 1958); and sportsman, explorer and former US ambassador in Colombo, Philip K Crowe, has an essay on

Male in his *Diversions of a Diplomat in Ceylon* (Van Nostram, New York, 1957).

Not much fiction has been set around the Maldives. There is only a sea adventure penned by Hammond Innes called *The Strode Venturer* (Collins, London, 1965). The setting of the story ranges from a London boardroom to the RAF bases on Gan and Addu atolls. The southern atoll's bid for independence in the early 1960s is worked into this adventure yarn. If you don't find it among Innes' other available paperbacks, there is a faded hardback copy in the National Library in Male.

Travel Guides

There are one-off glossy guides in several European languages published during the 1980s, as well as coffee-table photographic collections by German and Italian photographers.

A much more practical and down-to-earth guide is *Maldives* by Australian writer Stuart Bevan (Other People, Australia, 1987). Bevan spent five years on the islands, but is now persona non grata. The Maldivians took offence to some quips he made about prayer calls and the book is now unofficially banned.

Officially approved is *Papineau's Travel Guide to the Maldives* (MHP Publishing, Singapore, 1987). It's informative, has nice pics and a decent text but is not very practical.

Berlitz's tiny guide on Sri Lanka has an even tinier supplement on the Maldives.

The Islands of Maldives (Novelty, Male, 1983) written by the former director of the Department of Information, Hassan Ahmed Maniku, is more a list of the islands than a guidebook. Maniku attempts to sort out the eternal confusion of how many islands there are, what they are called and whether or not they are inhabited. Then he leaves it up to you to count them! The book has no pictures, illustrations or commentary.

Surprisingly, there are not many books

on the marine life or diving in the Maldives. *Land of 1000 Atolls* by Irenaeus Eibl-Eibesfeldt (World Publishing, New York, 1966) explores the underwater world around Nicobar and Maldive islands.

Bookshops

Male has several bookshops and two libraries but the range and access is limited.

Asrafee Bookshop on Orchid Magu, next to the Sri Lankan High Commission, is the only outlet for paperback fiction. It offers a small selection of western novels (as opposed to eastern; not Zane Grey and Louis Lamour).

Novelty Bookshop on Faridi Magu is better for Maldivian titles, some of which they publish. Again, there is not a large choice.

There are other bookshops but they deal only in school books and stationery.

Libraries

Half the books in the small collection at the National Library, on Majidi Magu in Male, came from the RAF Gan library when the British air base closed in 1976. The other half was appropriated from the estate of exiled former president Nasir. The selection is slowly being expanded although the library staff tend to buy up any new fiction the Asrafee Bookshop gets in.

The library is open daily except Fridays from 9 am to 12 noon and from 2 to 5 pm. Nonresidents can't borrow books, but are welcome to sit and read in the library.

Travellers and tourists can, however, borrow from the private Mohamed Ismail Didi (MID) Library on Ameer Ahmed Magu. It's open from 2 to 10 pm every day, except during Ramadan when it closes between 5.30 and 8 pm. You can join the library for Rf 12 with a monthly subscription of Rf 4. When borrowing books foreigners are required to leave Rf 100 as a deposit or their passport as security. 'The library shall hold itself responsible for the safe keeping of such documents', a notice promises.

The MID Library has a weird and wonderful assortment of literature including old editions of *National Geographic*, UN agency reports, soccer and cricket programmes, ancient press cuttings and magazines. There is also a good reference section for history and tourist books on the Maldives. It is worth visiting just to see the house, which is run by the son of the late M I Didi.

The British Voluntary Service Overseas (VSO) have a book exchange scheme. If you have any paperbacks you want to swap, contact their office (tel 323167) on Orchid Magu.

MAPS

Because of the scattered nature of the islands, the Maldives is a difficult country to map. If no-one has accurately counted the islands, it stands to reason that no-one has actually mapped them properly either.

Tourist maps of Male, the island and atoll, are available from the Department of Tourism office on Marine Drive. You don't need a map for the individual islands because they are so small.

The navigation charts are important and the British Admiralty is the best source. Failing that, try the Ministry of Fisheries in the Ghaazee Building, opposite the police station.

THINGS TO BUY

Just before the schools go back at the beginning of February, the government holds a craft fair in Male. Each atoll sends examples of its best work to the capital by dhoni. The quality pieces are sold in advance of the public opening to dignitaries, but remain on display until the end of the exhibition. There is still a large choice left, though the prices are higher than in the shops.

Gaddu and Fiyori islands in Gaaf Dhaal (South Huvadu Atoll) are the best sources of fine woven reed mats known as *kunaa*. They are naturally dyed with black and brown patterns and used as prayer mats or bed and chair covers. The *tundu kunaa* are special mats.

Red, black and yellow lacquer work is a feature of all sorts and sizes of wooden boxes, urns, walking sticks and other items. Baa (South Malosmadulu Atoll) always wins this category at the fair. Baa, particularly the capital island Eydafushi, is also known for making the traditional brown and cream *feli* cloth. It is difficult to find the cloth in Male shops as the locals there now prefer polyester from Singapore and Hong Kong. The felis I found for sale in Male were dusty and moth-eaten.

Alifushi, in Raa (North Malosmadulu Atoll), harbours the country's best boat-builders. They even export dhonis to other islands. Model dhonis come in all sizes, materials and prices. Just make sure you can get it home without breaking it.

It is worth looking around Male's tourist, craft and general shops for little caches of antique gold and silver jewellery. There seems to be the remnants of many a family heirloom scattered around, including heavy bracelets, rings, mesh belts, necklaces, and small, intricately engraved boxes. The price will depend on how enthusiastic you look and sound to the shopkeeper. Prepare yourself for a long bargaining session.

Ribudu Island in Dhaalu (South Nilandu Atoll) is famous for making gold jewellery, and Huludeli, in the same atoll, for silver jewellery. Old clocks and wooden chests feature prominently among other curios.

General household items which can make good souvenirs or gifts are anything made from a coconut shell, such as toddy holders and cups; woven palm leaf baskets; *sataa* mats; and folding, carved Koran rests.

Other popular souvenirs are sea shells, shark and dolphin teeth, or mother-of-pearl, coral and tortoiseshell goods. Laviyani (Fadippolu Atoll) is tops for making black coral and mother-of-pearl handicrafts.

I don't, however, recommend buying any of these shell and coral products, especially anything made of tortoiseshell. The turtles are supposed to be protected and the sale of shell products restricted, but the rules have little effect when money is involved. If tourists stop buying the products, however, maybe the reason for killing these creatures will be removed. Thankfully tortoiseshell products are a banned import in many countries, including Australia.

There is a nice line in dandy, concealed-dagger walking sticks. You'll have to pack it in your luggage when you leave the country, however, as you won't be allowed to class it as cabin baggage on a plane.

You can also buy the Maldives' national instrument, the bodu beru drum, but it is cumbersome to carry. The best ones come from Felidu, the capital island of Vaavu (Felidu Atoll). Check the drum skin to see if you might have trouble getting it past your own customs.

On a more mundane level, printed T-shirts are proving a lucrative sideline for Male souvenir shops and even some island fishing villages that are visited regularly by raiding parties of resort tourists. The shops and villages buy a batch of Chinese cotton T-shirts, dye on the designs and sell them for Rf 15. If you want your own motif on a shirt it'll cost you an extra Rf 10 to Rf 25.

The Maldives used to be a duty-free haven and Male was constantly overrun by plane loads of Indians and Sri Lankans on smuggling excursions. Although there is a new duty-free complex in Male, it is not worth buying luxury goods there. The Indians still come, though not in such great numbers, to buy polyester material for saris. They get it for a third of what they would pay back home.

In Male there are numerous tailors (one opposite the Nivico Guest House) who will stitch you a shirt in a day for Rf 15 (short sleeves) or Rf 20 (long sleeves). You need two metres of material, which will cost from around at Rf 10 per metre.

You can buy snorkelling, diving and fishing gear from the Shabim Emporium on Marine Drive, around the corner from the post office in Male. This place also stocks an alcohol-free range of perfumes, bulk-bought from Switzerland for Rf 24 a phial. The villagers use it for bathing; you might try adding a drop to your washing.

WHAT TO BRING

Despite the proliferation of palm leaves, the Maldivians are not great hat weavers, or even wearers. So make sure you bring some sort of head gear with you as protection against the sun because there aren't many hats for sale in the islands.

There is a slight drop in temperature during the night but not enough to warrant a thick jumper. Packing a light-weight sweater, however, is a good idea, and a waterproof cape or jacket is strongly advised, especially if you're not confined to a resort. Plastic bags can be useful for protecting clothes, cameras, documents and other items during sea journeys.

Backpacks are not the best way to carry your belongings. There are very few occasions when you'll do a lot of walking or have to carry your luggage too far. They also signal 'poor traveller' and you can kiss any chance of a permit goodbye.

Although nudity is forbidden it seems that in the resorts you can wear as little clothing as you like. In Male and other inhabited islands, however, travellers should make an effort not to offend or excite the townsfolk. Men should never go bare chested and women should wear skirts or shorts that cover their thighs.

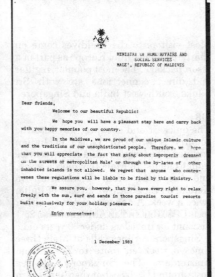

MINISTRY OF HOME AFFAIRS AND
SOCIAL SERVICES
MALE', REPUBLIC OF MALDIVES

Dear friends,

   Welcome to our beautiful Republic!

   We hope you will have a pleasant stay here and carry back with you happy memories of our country.

   In the Maldives, we are proud of our unique Islamic culture and the traditions of our unsophisticated people. Therefore, we hope that you will appreciate the fact that going about improperly dressed on the streets of metropolitan Male' or through the by-lanes of other inhabited islands is not allowed. We regret that anyone who contravenes these regulations will be liable to be fined by this Ministry.

   We assure you, however, that you have every right to relax freely with the sun, surf and sands in those paradise tourist resorts built exclusively for your holiday pleasure.

   Enjoy yourselves!

1 December 1983

Getting There

Most visitors to the Maldives come on chartered flights from Europe as part of a resort package. The most popular, regular and direct connections are with Sri Lanka, south-west India and Singapore.

AIR

The quickest and cheapest way into the country is with Air Lanka or Indian Airlines. The former runs a return service from Colombo to Male five days a week, and the latter from Trivandrum in Kerala, on the south-west coast of India, twice a week. A one-way ticket on either costs US$63 but Indian Airlines offers a 25% discount for travellers under 30 years old.

Singapore Airlines calls at Male three times a week en route to Zurich and Amsterdam. The Singapore/Male leg costs around US$280, but there is a return excursion fare for around US$450.

Singapore Airlines fly to the Maldives, via Singapore, from most of the state capitals in Australia. The one-way/return Melbourne/Singapore/Male fares, for example, are A$924/1251 in the low season, and A$1052/1553 in the high season.

Alitalia and Vienna's Lauda Air have both been operating one flight a week from Rome, but on a charter basis. Royal Nepal Airlines and Pakistan's PIA now fly to Male, and Malaysia's MAS is planning to start a service.

The only non-charter flight from London is with the United Arab Emirates airline, via Frankfurt and Dubai. There are no direct flights from the US or Australia. You must fly via Colombo, Singapore or Amsterdam for connections.

The other flying alternatives are the following charter lines: Balair from Zurich and Milan, Condor from Dusseldorf, Munich and Frankfurt, Monarch from London, Sterling from Stockholm and Copenhagen, and LTU from Dusseldorf and Munich. They each run two or three flights a week in the high season. With Condor you can purchase a one-way fare, but only in Germany.

Several of the European services stop en route at Bahrain or the United Arab Emirates to pick up western oil and construction workers heading for some R&R.

Airlines

Air Lanka (tel 323459) and Indian Airlines (tel 323003/4) have offices near each other on Marine Drive East in Male. Singapore Airlines (tel 324252) is on Faamudheyri Magu which runs parallel to and behind Chandani Magu.

All flight reservations are done through Air Maldives (tel 322436) at the Fashanaa Building on Marine Drive. They will give you a schedule of all flights in and out of Male. If you are not a resident of the Maldives, tickets must be paid for in US dollars.

Package Tours

Package holidays vary from one travel agent to another and from one month to the next, so check a few agents for the best deal. Some tour companies also offer a stopover in the Maldives, with Singapore Airlines, for two or more nights at a choice of resorts. It costs around US$50 per day which covers full-board and airport transfers.

About 90% of visitors to the Maldives go to just one resort on a 10 to 14 day package holiday where absolutely everything is arranged for them. These holidays begin at US$250 a week for full-board (airfares excluded). Discounts of up to 30% are offered during the low season and there are general reductions available on diving courses, fishing and watersports.

British tour companies offer a low season, 14 day holiday on Kuramathi, the largest and cheapest resort, for as little as £723 including flights and half-board.

In Australia, nine day packages from Sydney start at around A$1600/2000 for low/high season, on a twin share basis. It is cheaper from Perth.

There are also separate dhoni safari holiday packages to consider. These can be booked in advance or when you arrive in Male. World Expeditions, of Australia, offers a nine day sailing trip for A$933, excluding the flight to the Maldives.

Airport Arrival

Male International Airport is on Hulhule Island two km across the water from the capital. Customs, immigration and health checks are relatively perfunctory if you are on the way to a resort with all the other passengers, or if you pretend you are.

Flights are met by a gang of assorted tour operators and an even greater variety of ferries. There is a tourist information counter next to the bank, but don't count on either being open if you arrive after hours.

There will be tour agents and touts waiting for resort tourists but, if you're prepared to wait around until the crowds disperse, there may be one who will arrange a room for you in a Male guest house for US$15 a night or less. If not, take the ferry for Rf 5 across to the capital or, if you have the money, take a chance on a resort vacancy.

There is a public telephone at the airport. It costs Rf 1 to call Male but the line often breaks down.

Leaving the Maldives

Reaching the airport under your own steam is not quite as easy as leaving it. You have to allow plenty of time if you go by ferry, as they only run regularly at peak times, or you'll have to hire a ferry for around Rf 100. You could wait until there are enough people to share the cost. From 6.30 to 7.30 am you can usually travel free of charge to Hulhule on the ferries used by the airport staff.

If you are visiting other islands and depending on fishing dhonis allow a week to get back to Male and Hulhule.

There is a good cafe and restaurant at Hulhule (coffee Rf 4, toast, butter and jam Rf 10). In the departure lounge, there is a small duty-free and souvenir shop and a drinks counter.

Departure Tax Airport departure tax is US$7 and must be paid in that currency.

BOAT
Cargo Ship

Travelling to and from the Maldives by cargo ship is rarely done, but if you have time on your hands (and a lead-lined stomach) it is a possibility.

Several ships travel each month between Male and Colombo or Tuticorin, south of Trivandrum in south-west India, exporting fish and returning with spices, vegetables, biscuits and the like. In Tuticorin seek out Albert & Co shipping agents; and in Colombo ask for Cargo Boats Shipping Lanes.

Although no shipping agent seems to be enthusiastic about taking passengers, you

can try approaching ARU Enterprises on Orchid Magu in Male about passage to Tuticorin. Another place worth checking is Mariya Shipping on the same street.

If you're travelling to Sri Lanka, call first at Matrana Enterprises Ltd on Majidi Magu, Male (near the Olympus Cinema). They run an 800-tonne boat twice a month to Sri Lanka, via Gan Island. The voyage lasts from three to four days and they will take one to three passengers, depending on available space. The 'cabin' is an empty locker room with a mattress thrown in and the food is the basic curry and rice shared with the 15 crew. If you are hardy and still keen, the cost is US$35 or Rf 300 one way.

The Maldives Government operates two ships to Singapore, from where around 80% of the islands' imports come, but they do not carry passengers.

Yachts
Yachts, of course, present a more romantic but more remote opportunity. If you're looking for one in the Maldives, your best bet is to check with the Atolls Administration in Male where skippers must go to get cruising permits. But don't hold your breath.

If you arrive in the country by yacht, you must use the customs jetty on arrival and berth No 7 for disembarking. The regulations say: 'Foreigners are not allowed to land at Male without permission in the night after 10 pm'. Anchorage between Male and Funadoo Island is 'strictly prohibited'.

AIR

Air Maldives has one plane, an 18-seat Skyvan made by Short Brothers, Belfast. In a perfect world, it flies back and forth to Gan Island, in the southernmost Addu Atoll, three days a week and to Kadhu Island in Laamu twice a week. The flight to Kadhu costs US$43 or Rf 300.

The Gan flight is often fully booked well in advance and costs Rf 900 return, but nonresidents must pay in US dollars at the current rate of exchange. (Residents pay Rf 800.)

Air Maldives also runs a nine day package tour to Gan for US$680 which covers the flight and accommodation at the Gan Holiday Village (the former RAF barracks).

The two-hour flight to Gan provides a great opportunity for photographing the amazing array of islands and atolls. The steward hands out a soft drink and a sandwich or cake to passengers half way through the journey.

The sturdy little aircraft breaks down and goes to Singapore for servicing now and again. The timetable may also be disrupted by weather, official duties or extra flights added during school holidays and so on.

The alternative to Air Maldives is Inter Atoll Air (tel 322654) which operates a 20-seat seaplane on scheduled and charter flights between Hulule (Male) and many of the resorts. You can fly for as little as US$25 to the closer resorts on IAA's scheduled flights; or the minimum hourly or mileage charter cost is US$287.

SEA
Dhonis & Vedis

The *dhoni* (often spelt dorni) is the traditional all-purpose vessel of the Maldives. They come in all sizes and superstructures but are basically the same shape. (When they have the prow attached they look like ancient slave galleys.) Most are engine-powered, but only the ferries have done away with sails.

Fishing dhonis offer the best opportunity for rides to those atolls that are accessible within a day's journey from Male. For instance, Male to Felidu Island in Vaavu takes around six hours and costs Rf 50.

The departure time and duration of a voyage depends on the weather and sea conditions which vary considerably within and between the atolls. Be warned that this can make the trip exciting or terrifying, invigorating or sickening.

Fishing dhonis do not carry a radio, lifeboats or rescue gear. Capsize and you are history. This won't save your life, but if you wrap your luggage in a plastic bag it should protect your gear from getting wet on deck. You can buy giant, clear plastic bags from general stores on Majidi Magu in Male.

To travel to the outer atolls, you must

53

take a *vedi*. Vedis are larger, square-shaped wooden cargo boats used for trading between Male and the outer atolls. A trip down to Seenu (Addu Atoll), the most southerly and distant atoll, takes two days and costs Rf 85. Your bunk is a mat on a shelf, the toilet is the sea and fellow passengers may include chickens.

You will need a permit to persuade a dhoni or vedi skipper to take you to any island which is not a resort. If you have made any friends in Male they will usually introduce you to a fishing and supply boat from their island or atoll in Male harbour. But if you have to find your own, the vessels are identified by their atoll administrative letter marked within a square on the bow. These are:

Haa Alif	(A)	Meemu	(K)
Haa Dhaal	(B)	Faaf	(L)
Shaviyani	(C)	Dhaalu	(M)
Noonu	(D)	Thaa	(N)
Raa	(E)	Laamu	(O)
Baa	(F)	Gaaf Alif	(P)
Laviyani	(G)	Gaaf Dhaal	(Q)
Kaafu	(H)	Gnaviyani	(R)
Alif	(I)	Seenu	(S)
Vaavu	(J)		

Transport to Resorts around Male

There is a greater choice of vessel within Male (Kaafu) Atoll with regular supply and excursion dhonis running back and forth from nearby resorts to the capital.

The closest resorts to the capital and therefore the cheapest to visit are Kurumba, Bandos and Furana. You can telephone the resort or contact its Male office to find out times, costs and conditions. Fares range from US$10 to US$20 return. For the more distant resorts you will have to stay a night or two if there are vacancies.

You can get a free transfer to Furana, the Australian-owned resort, by catching their supply boat on a Saturday, Monday or Wednesday. It leaves Furana at 2 pm and returns between 4.30 and 5 pm.

The United Nations club run a day trip to a nearby resort each Friday, weather permitting, at a nominal fee. It is supposed to be for UN staff, expats and guests but there's no harm in asking. You can call the UNDP (tel 324501/2/3) or go to their offices on Kulhidoshu Magu.

Finally you can charter a covered dhoni from the Nasandhura Palace Hotel side of

Marine Drive by bargaining with individual boat owners or through a boat hire agency.

ZSS (tel 322505) Marine Drive, hire speedboats (up to five passengers) or covered dhonis (maximum 20 people). The return fare to Kurumba is Rf 275/150 (fast/slow boat); Bandos Rf 375/200; Cocoa Rf 700/350; and Kudahithi Rf 800/400. You can also hire the dhoni at Rf 50 an hour with crew. The rates are similar for private hire.

For more distant resorts, you may have to go to the airport to catch boats waiting to transfer tourists off incoming flights. Check plane arrival times first.

Dhoni Cruises

If you only have a week or two to spend in the Maldives and want to get around, this is the best way. A few tour companies offer cruises around the atolls neighbouring Male. They charge from US$45 to US$65 per person per day all-inclusive aboard a cabin dhoni.

The operator arranges the permits to visit approved island villages. You sleep on board or camp out on uninhabited islands.

Trips usually last a week and cater for six to 10 people. Voyages Maldives (tel 322019, 323017) on Faridi Magu, are well recommended. They go to Vaavu or Alif (Felidu or Ari atolls) in the south and Laviyani (Fadippolu Atoll) in the north.

Rover Tours (tel 323537), at 10 Ever Glory, and Altaf Enterprises (tel 323378), in Majidi Bazaar, offer cheaper 'safari' cruises for up to six people. In some cases diving is available for little extra cost.

You can book these through the adventure tour operators in Australia, Europe and USA.

Yacht Cruises

After going through customs at Male, private yachts need to apply for a Cruising Permit from the Atolls Administration. Apart from resort visits, you must sleep on board.

According to one yachtsman, the Maldives are comparatively awkward to sail around. He said it is difficult to anchor in the deep water surrounding most islands and the resorts don't welcome yachts.

ROAD

Car

There are motor vehicles only on Male and Addu Atoll. Apart from two 'experimental' paved streets in the capital, the road network is compressed coral, sand and earth.

The roads flood easily after heavy rain, turning into rivers full of hidden potholes. Maldivians are supposed to drive on the left-hand side of the road, but in practice the go around the potholes any which way they can and the cars rarely get out of second gear. There is, however, a major reconstruction project underway to seal the roads.

Thanks to the RAF, who flew away for good in 1976, Addu Atoll has some paved roads but they are in a bad shape.

Cars are status symbols and traffic congestion is a problem in Male. The government has slapped a 200% import tax on cars to reduce the influx. If you borrow a private car, you first have to get your licence approved by the Department of Transport.

Taxi

Taxi services operate on both Male and Addu, but are only necessary to get to and from the airport boats. You can walk around most islands in less than an hour.

A taxi in Male costs Rf 70 an hour or Rf 20 a trip. Call Regular Taxis (tel 322454), Express (tel 323132).

Motorcycle & Bicycle

Motorcycles are becoming more popular, though a greater curse, in the Maldives. Those who can't afford the motor just have a bicycle.

There are about 14,000 bicycles on Male. It's fun to see Maldivians riding their bikes in the rain and almost disappearing into hidden potholes amid hoots of laughter from their friends.

There are no motorcycles or bicycles for hire on an official basis. Private hire of a bicycle costs between Rf 60 and Rf 100 a month. Make sure there is a *bati* (light) fitted on front. They're Chinese-made and cost only Rf 10 each. The light must be on at 6 pm whether it's dark or not. If it doesn't work, keep tapping it in case you pass a police officer. They are overzealous in enforcing the rules which include arresting you for merely walking the bike the wrong way up a one-way street.

To add to the fun, or confusion, the one-way and no-entry signs are sited in an uncertain way at intersections and you're never sure which street they apply to.

RESORT OPERATORS

Each resort has an office or agency in Male. The main operators are:

Universal Enterprises
    38 Orchid Magu (tel 322971) and Marine Drive East. They run Baros, Fesdu, Kuramathi, Kurumba, Veligandu Huraa, and Nakachafushi resorts.
Safari Tours
    Chandani Magu (tel 323524). They run Dhiggiri, Alimatha, Boduhithi, Ellaidu and Kudahithi resorts.
Dhirham Travels
    Faamudheyri Magu (tel 323372). They run Gasfinolhu, Fihalhohi and Vabbinfaru.
Treasure Island
    Marine Drive East (tel 322165). They run Furana, Bathala, Mayaafushi and Leisure Island.

The agents for the other resorts are given in the Atoll to Atoll chapter when the resort island is discussed.

TOUR OPERATORS

Perhaps most important for the unattached traveller are the few independent agencies.

Of these Rover Tours (tel 323537), 10 Ever Glory in Male, could prove very helpful – if the chief partner Mohammed Arif has managed to last the pace. When last seen Arif was trying to meet every flight into the islands to help place independent visitors in resorts, hotels or guest houses. He was the only operator who aimed to help individual travellers. When I arrived at 3 am he arranged the ferry, the accommodation booking and accompanied me to a good guest house – all for no more than the US$10 it cost for the room.

He claimed to be able to get rooms in certain resorts for rates similar to those offered to airline staff and travel agents. He was also offering 10% discounts to students and even helping out travellers who had run out of money. Hopefully he hasn't gone out of business or, just as bad for us, gone up market.

Imad Agency (tel 322964), 39/2 Chandani Magu, may be worth trying, to find out about special deals. Voyages Maldives (tel 322019, 323017), on Faridi Magu, have reasonable deals, as well as representing Balair, Sterling and Monarch charters. They are the specialists in dhoni safari cruises.

Travellers in search of a desert island paradise will be slightly disappointed in Male.

The island capital is packed to the edges with nearly 50,000 residents. To help accommodate everyone, the boundaries of the island have been extended twice over the past 30 years through land reclamation. Despite the population density on one single square mile, Male never strikes you as over-crowded or bustling. It's more like a small town, neatly laid out and tidy; although it's developing at a fast rate and losing a little of its character with each new building. The first five-storey building, an office block, was built in 1987.

Since freewheeling visitors may have to spend some time here getting organised and cleared for inter-atoll travel, it is worth getting to know the place and people well.

Orientation

As well as expanding, Male (pronounced Mah-lee) is changing rapidly with constant rebuilding. Government and commercial offices shift around and new developments spring up. As it only takes 30 minutes to walk from one end of the island to the other, the inconvenience is minimal.

The capital is divided into four districts, from west to east: *Maafannu*, which covers most of the western end of the island from the Singapore Bazaar area of Chandani Magu, is where you'll find the Theemuge (president's home), a few embassies, guest houses and the residential areas of Male's poorer citizens; *Machangolhi*, which runs east-west across the middle of the island, boasts the popular cafes and restaurants of Majidi Magu, the district's main street; *Galolhu*, a crowded residential maze in the south-east part of Male, is a confusing and interesting place to explore; and *Henveiru*, the north-east pocket of Male, is renowned for the beautiful houses of the *befalu* (upper class) along Ameer Ahmed Magu and the fine buildings on Marine Drive overlooking the harbour.

Magu is the Maldivian word for a wide, unpaved coral street. A *goalhi* is a narrow lane, and a *higun* is a longer, wider goalhi.

Business activity on Male is weighted towards the north end of the island, around Marine Drive and the harbours. The other principal streets are Chandani Magu, which divides Male from north to south, and Majidi Magu, which divides it from east to west.

The fishing and cargo port is to the west of Chandani Magu, the tourist and yacht harbour to the east. The reclaimed land is mainly to the south.

Information

For information on foreign consulates, bookshops, libraries, telephones, hospitals and pharmacies refer to the Maldives' Facts for the Visitor chapter.

Tourist Offices There is a tourist office on Marine Drive, near Air Lanka, where you can get maps, books and limited tourist literature. The head office of the Department of Tourism, in the Ghaazee Building on Ameer Ahmed Magu, would be more useful for specific enquiries.

The Atolls Administration office, where you must get permits to visit uninhabited islands, is next to Air Maldives in the Fashanaa Building on Marine Drive.

Voyages Maldives is on Faridi Magu east of the Novelty Bookshop. For the addresses of other resort operators and travel agents refer to the Getting Around chapter.

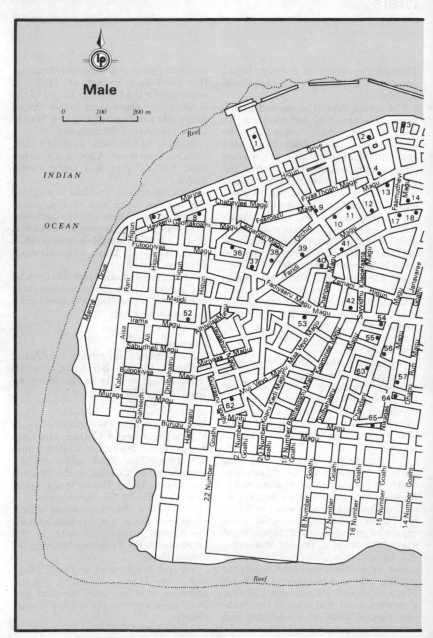

Male

INDIAN

OCEAN

Reef

Reef

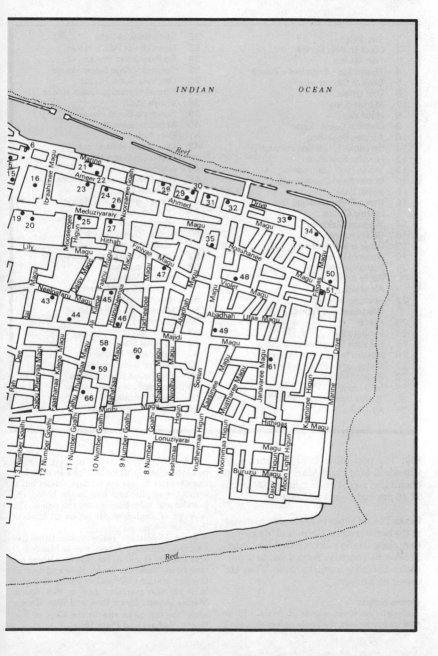

1	Customs	32	State Bank of India
2	Local Trading Centre	33	Nasandhura Palace Hotel
3	Fish Market	34	Gadhoo Guest House
4	Theemuge – President's Palace	35	Seemaa Village Guest House
5	Bank of Ceylon	36	Oak Villa Guest House
6	Post Office	37	Fehivid Huvaruge Guest House
7	Mermaid Inn	38	British VSO
8	Hotel Alia	39	Sunshine Guest House
9	Dheraha Guest House	40	Maafaru Guest House
10	Asrafee Bookshop	41	Ever Pink
11	Sri Lankan High Commission	42	Downtown Restaurant
12	Novelty Bookshop	43	Green Lin Guest House
13	Indian High Commission	44	National Library
14	Ocean Reed Guest House	45	Post & Telecommunications Centre
15	Habib Bank	46	Olympus Cinema
16	Grand Friday Mosque & Islamic Centre	47	Three Lights Guest House
17	Voyages Maldives	48	USA Consulate
18	Gelato Italiano	49	Hospital
19	Cable & Wireless	50	Maagiri Guest House
20	National Museum & Sultan Park	51	Aazaadhuge Guest House
21	Fashanaa Building – Atolls Administration & Air Maldives	52	Lead House Guest House
		53	Indian Restaurant
22	Ghaazee Building – Department of Tourism	54	Bank of Maldives
		55	Noomas Guest House
23	Police	56	Nivico Guest House
24	Immigration	57	Mazaage Guest House
25	Sakeena Manzil Guest House	58	Fototeknik
26	Hukuru Miski – Old Mosque	59	Selvio Guest House
27	Muleeaage – President's Office	60	National Stadium
28	Bank of Maldives	61	Sony Guest House
29	MID Library	62	Velagoli Guest House
30	Tourist Information Office	63	Koosheege Guest House
31	Air Lanka	64	Araarootuge Guest House
		65	Kendnifashuige Guest House
		66	Alafaru Guest House

Post The post office is at the corner of Chandani Magu and Marine Drive. It is open daily, except Friday, from 7.30 am to 12.45 pm and from 4 to 5.50 pm.

Banks The six banks in Male are clustered at the harbour end of Chandani Magu and east along Marine Drive. They are open Sunday to Thursday from 9 am to 1 pm, and on Saturday from 9 to 11 am. They are closed on Fridays.

House Names

Although the street names in Male will be strange to your ears, the house names shouldn't be. The Maldivians seem to have a great passion for bestowing an English name on their homes. Most houses are modest abodes but it seems the smaller and plainer the house, the grander and more flamboyant the name. The selection of English words covers all kinds of images.

Some Maldivians prefer rustic titles like Crabtree, Hillman, Forest and G Meadow (I presume the G stands for Green). Others are specifically floral like Sweet Rose and Luxury Garden. Marine titles and anything with blue in it are also popular, such as Sea Speed, Marine Dream, Dawn Dive and Blue Haven, while the sun gives rise to the likes of Sun Dance, Radiant and Plain Heat.

Perhaps, in that respect, the best attractions are Thor Heyerdahl's recent archaeological discoveries of stone figures and carvings from pre-Muslim civilisations, which feature in his book *The Maldive Mystery*.

The Maldivians, however, do not seem to be so proud of the relics. They are on display but are tucked away in a side room without any identification labels or numbers.

The park surrounding the museum was once part of the grounds of the sultan's palace. It is small but on the crowded, compact, treeless island, it is an oasis. It would be a nice place to spend a quiet hour reading or writing but it's only open to the public on Fridays.

There are also exotic ones like Paris Villa, River Nile and Aston Villa, but I liked the more esoteric Remind House, Pardon Villa and Mary Lightning, or those that sound like toilet disinfectants – Ozone, Green Zest and Frenzy.

Shop names, on the other hand, are straight to the point – Kleen Laundry, Fair Price, Goodwill and Neat Store.

National Museum & Sultan Park

This small, two-storey museum is open daily, except government holidays, from 9 am to noon and from 3 to 6 pm. Entry is Rf 5. The entrance is guarded by a WW I German torpedo, donated by a Royal Navy warship.

You'll be followed rather than guided by a caretaker who makes sure you don't touch or take anything. Exhibits consist mainly of the sultans' belongings – threadbare clothes, weapons and throne. These exhibits are poorly labelled and, as the museum staff speak only Dhivehi, there is no-one to explain the story or significance behind them.

Islamic Centre & Grand Friday Mosque

Built in 1984 with help from the Gulf States, Pakistan, Brunei and Malaysia, this *miski* (mosque) dominates the sprouting Male skyline. The first thing you see when sailing towards the capital is its gold dome glinting in the sun. (The gold is actually anodised aluminium.) The *munnaaru*, or minaret, is the tallest structure in Male.

Visits to the Grand Friday Mosque must be arranged around prayer times and between 9 am and 5 pm. The mosque closes to non-Muslims 15 minutes before prayer and for the following hour. Before noon and between 2 and 3 pm are the best times to visit.

Invading bands of resort tourists and casual sightseers are not encouraged but if you are genuinely interested and suitably dressed, you'll get in. You will be asked to remove your shoes and to wash your feet in the huge ablution blocks. Do not wear shorts or short dresses to visit the mosque.

Once inside the mosque, someone will accompany you to the prayer hall which can accommodate up to 6000 worshippers and has beautiful carved wooden side panels and doors.

The centre also includes a conference hall, library and classrooms.

Hukuru Miski

In order to visit nearby Hukuru Miski, the oldest mosque in the country, you have to apply to the Department of Religious Affairs (tel 322266) for permission.

Built in 1656, the mosque is famed for its intricate carvings. One long panel, actually carved in the 13th century, commemorates the introduction of Islam to the Maldives by Abu Al Barakat in 1153 AD.

Apparently worshippers have to face the corner of this mosque when kneeling to pray because the foundations face the sun instead of Mecca!

In the graveyard of Hukuru Miski, overlooked by the imposing blue and white *munnaaru*, is the tomb of Abu Al Barakat adorned with medieval pennons (flags) and protected by a coral wall. The gold-plated tombstones mark the graves of former sultans.

There are more than 20 *miskis*, often little more than a coral building with an iron roof, scattered around Male. Hukuru Miski, near the Grand Friday Mosque, is on Meduziyaraiy Magu.

Singapore Bazaar

This is the nickname given to the conglomeration of stores along, and around the bottom end of, Chandani Magu (the main north-south street), probably because Singapore is where they get most of their items for sale. Souvenir shops seem to propagate here, but there is also an atmospheric (smelly) cluster of outlets trading in spices, dried fish, metal bits and rope.

Cannons

An interesting diversion (or excuse for a walk around Male's coastline) is to see how many ancient cannons you can spot. There are some embedded on the fishing boat dock on Marine Drive and piles of them on the rocks along the eastern end of the island.

The cannons are the only remnants of the ignominious 15 year occupation of Male by the Portuguese. Their brutal regime came to an end in 1573 when the great hero Thakurufaan and his two brothers led a Maldivian raid on the foreign garrison, killing everyone within.

Places to Stay – bottom end

Guest houses that cost less than US$10 a night tend to be transit stops for Sri Lankan resort workers or dosshouses for groups of Indians and Sri Lankans on a quick small business raid. Each room contains three or more beds and it's not uncommon for people to cook on the floor in the room.

There are two of these places, however, which are recommended for being 'reasonably clean' and very friendly.

The *Fehivid Huvaruge* (tel 324470) at 3 Funa Goalhi, near where Faridi Magu joins Orchid Magu, has five rooms and 18 beds. The proprietor, Ahmed Busree, charges US$8 a night. Breakfast and meals are an extra US$2 and US$3. The toilet and well are communal.

The second place, nearby, is the *Sunshine Guest House* (tel 322336) at 26 Faridi Magu. It is run by Busree's friend Ibrahim Rasheed. It also has five rooms and a score of beds for US$11 in the low season and US$15 in the high season. Meals are not available. Rasheed also organises trips to islands, and fishing and diving tours.

Not too far away, south-west of Majidi Magu, but not such good value is *Lead House* (tel 322310) on Irama Magu. The three double rooms each cost US$14 per night. There are no meals, but you can play table tennis there.

The *Ocean Reed* (tel 323311), opposite Gelato Italiano on Faridi Magu, has five rooms with a communal shower and toilet. It's quite central but being next to the Singapore Bazaar means it's also quite noisy. The owner, Hassan Abbas, charges US$15 a night, meals included.

Opposite the US Consulate, at 15 Violet Magu (off Sosun Magu), is *Nayaa Bahaaru* (tel 322886). It has five uninspiring rooms for US$8 a night, but the family will give you a kind reception.

The *Mazaage* (tel 324669), on Nikagas Magu, offers several dark and dank ground floor rooms for US$15 a night with breakfast. They have a video recorder.

A block north of Majidi Magu, at 6 Neeloafaru Magu, is the *Green Lin* (tel 322279). It has five rooms and is popular with Indian visitors. I found the manager helpful but the owner surly. You can pay a basic US$11 per night, or US$20 a night will get you meals and free trips to nearby islands.

Places to Stay – middle

'If the hotels are too expensive and the rest not good enough welcome to Mermaid Inn.' This business card inscription just about sums it up for the Mermaid Inn and other guest houses in the US$15 and over range.

The pink-painted *Mermaid Inn* (tel 323329), at the west end of Marine Drive overlooking the harbour, used to have a liquor licence but is no longer an inn. Managed by Seasun Tours, it has two single and eight double or triple rooms. They are clean, smartly furnished, carpeted and have attached bathrooms. A single costs US$20 per night. Seasun also offers US$30 or Rf 150 return trips to Furana resort, and full-board accommodation on a range of resorts from US$40/45 a single/double per day in the low season.

The best value in this price range is the *Nivico* (tel 322942) on Chandani Magu, above a small general store. For US$15, you get a large double bedroom with your own clean shower and toilet. The manager and shopkeeper, Ibrahim Rasheed, is very helpful.

Should the Nivico's seven rooms be occupied, you will be referred to the less informal but equally good *Araaruotuge*, overlooking the school on Madhoshi Goalhi (near the corner of Nikagas Magu); or to the much smaller *Alidhooge* (tel 322649) on Zamani Higun. These two cost US$20 a night, including breakfast. Doubles are US$35.

Smaller than the Mermaid Inn, but similar in price and standard, is the *Sony* (tel 323249) on Janavaree Magu. It has six rooms for US$20 per night and is popular with visiting sports teams. On the same street is the Evening Glory cafe and the Crest cafe.

Another old favourite is the *Aazaadhuge* (tel 322095) at 4 Roashanee Magu, near the north-east coast of Male. It is run by the amiable Kuda Thuthu who charges US$15 per person. Until the government clampdown, he used to operate dhoni and camping trips to the islands. Now he takes in teachers and is likely to be full all year, except during the holidays from 22 December to 30 January, but he's still a good contact.

Around the corner, on Marine Drive next to the Nasandhura Palace Hotel, is the clean and airy *Gadhoo* (tel 323222/3) which costs US$20/30 for single/double accommodation with breakfast. There are three double rooms with attached bathrooms.

Not so appealing is the *Sakeena Manzil* (tel 323281) on Meduziyaraiy Magu. This place is sort of sandwiched between the Hukuru Miski and the Grand Friday Mosque which assures guests of early, regular wake-up calls. Even though meals are included, the Sakeena Manzil is overpriced at US$25 per night for a single. The dormitory-style rooms have several beds packed close together. The proprietor said he separated Asian and western guests! He also organises tours.

The *Ranmahi* (tel 323362) on Lonuziyarai Magu, behind the national stadium on the south side, has four small triple rooms with attached bathrooms for US$15. The owner is an authorised moneychanger.

Places to Stay – top end
The *Maagiri* guest house on Roashanee Magu has singles/doubles for US$30/40 including breakfast.

The next two hotels may be top end in price but certainly not in standard, however they do have the only bars and licensed restaurants in Male and are good meeting places.

Although long-awaited renovations are underway, the single-storey *Nasandhura Palace* (tel 323380) is anything but a palace. Because it is close to the airport it relies heavily on arriving and departing tourist parties. Rooms with air-con cost US$55/75 for a single/double including breakfast. The restaurant menu is à la carte.

There is little to choose between the Palace and the *Hotel Alia* (tel 322080) at the other end of Marine Drive on Haveeru Higun. There singles/doubles cost US$56/83, breakfast is US$3 and dinner or lunch is US$7. They also charge US$5 during the day and US$7 at night for airport transfers.

In the courtyard of the Alia is a tiny pond full of turtles. They should be in the sea, but have a look at them first if you're thinking of buying anything made from their shells. Hopefully it will put you off the idea.

The bar at the Alia is called the *Oasis*, and for many an expat it is just that. Don't, however, feel obliged to match the regular patrons drink for drink. Guest workers get a liquor allowance of 60 beers a month or the equivalent value of anything else, which means cut-price booze at either the Alia or the Nasandhuru. They pay Rf 6 for a can of Singapore Lion or Heineken. You pay the full Rf 10 for a can of beer, Rf 12 for a whisky and Rf 15 for other spirits. You can also pay in US dollars. The bars are normally open till 11 pm.

Finally there is the *Sosunge* (tel 323025) on Sosun Magu, which was a government guest house until it was renovated and reopened as hotel. I was told, however,

that it costs US$400 a single and US$500 a double for the privilege of spending a night in one of the four bedrooms. If you stay there let us know what it's like.

Places to Eat
There are three sorts of places to eat in Male – cafes or tearooms, small European-style restaurants or cafes, and hotels.

Resort rates are all full-board, but you can visit the resorts near Male for meals only. Lunch or dinner cost around Rf 50, snacks Rf 20 and coffee Rf 10.

Cafes There must be a hundred cafes in Male and you'll find them on almost every street. They open as early as 5 am and close as late as 1 am, particularly around the port area where they cater for fishermen. Although many are called the something 'hotel', they do not offer accommodation in any form.

As far as the Maldivians are concerned, cafes are male domains, but foreign women are not hassled or refused service. They are just stared at.

The cafes are all similar in decor, service and price. Personal preferences will depend on factors such as proximity to your guest house or who is serving and managing the place. A good meal costs around Rf 15.

The cafes close their doors for 15 minutes at prayer times but if you're already inside, there's no problem. You won't have to stop talking or eating or anything and they certainly won't throw you out.

On the tables you will find a selection of sweet and savoury titbits called *hedhikaa*, which include small bowls of rice pudding, tiny bananas, wobbly gelatin pieces of indeterminate colour and taste, curried fish cakes, and frittered dough balls which are sometimes empty, sometimes filled.

Meals include omelettes, soups, curried fish, roshi (unleavened bread) and sauce. The Maldivians cut up the roshi, mix it in

Top: 'Antique & Style' Male (PS)
Bottom: Temporary Fish Market Male (RW)

Top: Male Harbour (PS)
Bottom: Portuguese cannon and mooring point (RW)

Top: Dhoni (WE)
Bottom: Palms in the sunset at Hitadu (RW)

Top: The Boiling Fish & Shark Hotel (RW)
Left: The main street in Maradu (RW)
Right: Young waiter outside the Target Point Hotel Maradu (RW)

a bowl and have it for breakfast. Don't mistake it for cereal, as I did one morning.

A cup of *sa*, which is sweet white tea, or a glass of sweet flavoured milk (powdered or condensed) always accompanies meals and is served instantly by one of two or three scurrying young waiters. There is no coffee but you can order your tea black; and just say *hakuru naala sa* if you want it without sugar.

Tea costs Rf 2 and the hedhikaa are Rf 1 to Rf 3. Help yourself to the prepared selection on your table which is replenished when you leave. The waiter totals up what you have eaten and writes the amount on a scrap of paper. Pay him or the man at the door.

My favourite cafes were the *Mujeedhee Uafaa* and the neighbouring *Junction Hotel*, at the corner of Majidi and Chandani magus. In the centre of town on Faridi Magu, just along from Voyages Maldives, is the *Fareedhee Uafaa*. The popular *Moon Cafe* is opposite the banks on Orchid Magu, and in the small lane behind is the *Hotel Daan Buma*.

Hotel de Shark cafe, Male

Around the corner from the banks is the *Hilton*, an up-market cafe by Maldivian standards. They have a restaurant upstairs which offers a range of curries with rice, side dishes and tea for as little as Rf 10.

Nearby, and closer to the harbour, is the aptly named *Dawn Cafe* which is busy very early in the morning. On Marine Drive near the Nasandhura Hotel is the *Queen of the Night* which caters for the night owls.

The *Hotel Dunthari*, on Majidi Magu near the Bank of Maldives, and the *Evening Glory* and *Crest Hotel* on Janavaree Magu are worth a checking out. Try the *Hotel de Shark* next door to the *Boiling Fish House* as well. It's opposite the miski on Dhilbahaaru Higun in the north-west quarter of town.

Western-style Restaurants There are two basic types of western-style restaurants – day parlours and night spots. Day parlours are popular with tourist parties from the resorts.

Gelato Italiano, on the corner of Faridi and Chandani magus, is a popular day parlour. It specialises in ice cream sundaes ranging in price from Rf 22 to Rf 100, soft drinks for Rf 10 and little else. However, they do make the best cup of coffee in the country for Rf 5. Tables are outside on a sand floor, under a thatched roof. Watch out for mosquitoes feeding on your legs.

Hidden in the lane next to the Habib Bank on Chandani Magu is a much cheaper alternative. It is decked out as a Wild West cantina but for some strange reason is called *Top Cream*. When I was there they played a cassette tape of horses snorting and galloping! Coke, 7-Up or an ice cream cone costs only Rf 4.

Further up Chandani Magu, overlooking the tennis courts and the Male Indoor Sports Centre, is the *Canteen*. You can watch Male's up and coming tennis pros over an ice cream and Coke.

The dinner spots are mostly on Majidi

Magu. They all try to be small, candlelit and intimate, but sometimes turn out to be cold, gloomy and loud. You can get a three course meal for under Rf 50.

The most established restaurant is *Downtown*. This is the place where young Male males take their girlfriends to woo and impress them, and where diplomats, government officials and voluntary workers go to relax. The main complaint is the limited selection of background music; they play the same tape over and over again. The menu includes tomato soup, mixed salad, curry, steak & chips, ice cream and coffee.

Directly across the road is *Quench* which has both indoor and outdoor tables under a thatched roof. The menu includes hamburgers, egg & chips, spaghetti, sandwiches and fruit juice. They also do Indian meals.

The decor of *Island Foods*, near the national stadium, is unadorned concrete and the atmosphere is close to that of a bomb shelter. The sugar that should be in the cakes is concentrated in the coffee.

The only Indian restaurant in Male is on Majidi Magu and, just in case there is any confusion, it is called *Indian Restaurant*. There is a good restaurant on Marine Drive called the *New Pot*.

Self-Catering The Local Trading Centre, behind the fishing harbour on Haveeru Higun is the best place to buy what little fruit is grown in the country. Prices vary with the seasons.

The modern alternative, complete with close-circuit cameras and turnstiles, is the Green & Fresh Supermarket opposite the Top Cream cafe on Chandani Magu. It stocks imported fruit and vegetables as well as tinned versions.

There's also a good grocery shop called Sanco Fresh opposite the Nivico guest house on Chandani Magu. I bought an Australian orange and a packet of Indian biscuits there. The fish market is next door on Marine Drive.

Entertainment

There may be no nightclubs, dance halls or discos in town but Male is a surprisingly lively place from about 8 pm to late in the evening. Majidi Magu is as busy as Oxford St with late-night shoppers and cafes full of people, while music and general family commotion spills over the walls of every house.

For the traveller, the only real entertainment choices are dining out, going to the cinema or drinking at the hotel bars. There are four cinemas, the *Olympus, National, Star* and *Bukharie*, which show three hour Hindi sagas or B-grade action adventures in English. Occasionally a reputable feature is shown.

The theatres, however, are under threat from the increasing popularity of video cassette recorders. There are numerous video outlets and some guest houses have VCRs. Tape rental is Rf 15 a night. Any sexual or violent scenes may have been censored.

'Cultural' exhibitions are sometimes put on at the Olympus cinema or in the schools, but not on a regular or commercial basis.

Except during holidays and festivals the only daytime diversions are football and cricket matches, often against teams from Sri Lanka, at the National Stadium on Majidi Magu. Tickets cost Rf 7 or Rf 10 for centre seats with a better view. There are no water sports to speak of around Male.

The Atolls

The Maldives is a collection of 26 atolls, listed in this chapter from north to south, firstly by the administrative title and secondly by the traditional name. The letter in brackets is the administrative code letter by which fishing dhonis are identified, and the distance noted is from Male to the atoll capital.

Before you visit any inhabited atoll, other than a resort, you must have a permit from the Ministry of Atolls Administration in Male. (Refer to the Permits section in the Facts for the Visitor chapter.)

The capital island is often not the largest in population or size, but it houses the atoll office. This is where you can radio-telephone any local person in the atoll and where you must present your permit. It is staffed by the atoll secretary or deputy chief (if the atoll chief is not around), and a radio operator. Each island has a kateeb (island chief), an island administrative office and a court. Contact with other islands in the atoll is by CB radio.

The lifestyle on most of the islands is fairly similar and it would be difficult to pick which ones to visit, if indeed the choice was offered. Gnaviyani (Fuamulaku) and Seenu (Addu Atoll) in the south are definitely worth considering. The only registered places to stay and eat apart from the resorts are on Seenu.

Allow plenty of time to travel to and from any island, especially if you have an international flight to catch in Male. The availability of transportation depends on when the fishermen come and go, which in turn depends on the weather and how much fish, money, or supplies are needed. It's a different story of course if you're on a package staying at the resorts because transfers are arranged around international and domestic flight arrivals and departures.

Uninhabited islands are those which have vegetation and presumably could be, or have been, inhabited. They do not include the hundreds, if not thousands, of precarious tiny coral islets and sandbanks scattered around and between the islands.

RESORTS

A word or two on the 59 resorts. Like the villages or islands themselves, there is little to choose between them, and if you come on a package holiday the choice is limited to six or less.

Except for those in the 'you have to be a millionaire to stay there' bracket, resorts are not noted for their cuisine, or ironically, their solitude. You may be isolated on the tiny isle for most of the holiday, but in the high season you might also be stuck there with 100 or more other tourists.

Most of the resorts are centred around the capital island of Male in Kaafu (North Male Atoll). New ones will continue to open in Alif (Ari Atoll), where a dozen are under construction. The government is planning to hand some of the resort islands back to the people, to ease the overpopulation on Male, but this may be wishful thinking because the economy depends so much on the tourist dollar.

Accommodation is generally in thatched bungalows, cabanas, bures, rondavels, units, huts or whatever the brochure wants to call them, with an attached bathroom and shower, and a verandah of sorts usually facing the beach. Only about seven resorts have two-storey accommodation.

The standard resort recreations are diving, snorkelling, dhoni sailing, windsurfing, water-skiing, volleyball, badminton, tennis, table tennis, day/night fishing, discos, videos, cultural shows (ie bodu beru), island hopping (including Male if the resort is close enough), souvenir stores, libraries, and board games.

Several resorts, including Kanifinolhu, Bandos and Kurumba, have been upgraded. This was mostly because of the sudden influx of Japanese tourists who expected more for their yen.

One of the major complaints, after the one about the ordinary food, is the salty bore water showers. Almost all of the resorts used to pump the water from the ground and filter it through sand. Sometimes it was heated, which resulted in a pungent smell, but mostly it was (is) left cold. The water is never freezing of course, but it is difficult to wash in as soap and shampoo won't lather. (Unless you use Shower Gel you end up with stiff and sticky hair.)

So, about half the resorts now have desalinisation plants and others collect rain water in barrels. Some provide fresh water 24 hours a day, while some restrict it to a few hours in the evening. Occasionally the desalinisation systems break down or there are long periods without rain; then it's back to the bore water and sea water.

There are, however, always flasks of fresh drinking water in the rooms and at meals.

Rates

All rates quoted are the 'fixed individual tariff ' (FIT) for one day/night full-board in the low season. The price increases for the high season vary remarkably from resort to resort. In some cases it's only a matter of a few more dollars, in others the rate more than doubles.

You will get cheaper rates through overseas packages and with the independent tour operators in Male, some of whom are connected with guest houses. There are also some excellent 'special offers' and stopover deals during the low season. Refer to the Getting There chapter and try a couple of travel agents at home to compare prices.

Resorts fall into low, medium and high price ranges. The following rates are for the low season which lasts from May to September. The bottom range starts from US$25/40 a night for single/double on a full-board basis. The middle range for singles/doubles begins at US$45/60 and the top range at US$80/100.

The bottom range resorts are Eriyadu, Fihalhohi, Helengeli, Hembadu, Kanduma, Kuramathi, Little Hura, Lhohifushi, Olhuveli and Ziyaaraifushi.

There may be extra charges for air-con and it's a good idea to check what recreational facilities are included in the cost. Diving, for instance, is rarely included in the package although you may get a free introductory dive.

Also remember that each resort charges a boat transfer for taking you to and from Hulhule Airport. This starts at US$10 for the closer islands and goes up to US$75 or US$100 for the more distant ones. Generally children under two years old travel free and those up to 12 years for half price.

So before booking a resort you should find out whether the resort has the following:

fresh water
hot water
a proper chef or a glorified can-opener
international clientele or mainly German or Italian groups
a full range of activities and facilities, and which ones are included in the full-board rates
a good diving school

If it is difficult to find more information than this guide book provides, it may suggest that the resort is used exclusively by European tour operators such as Club Vacanze or Jet Reisen. The Male contact number and address listed should provide such information. There are continual changes among the contact people, some of whom are owners or operators while others are merely agents.

Diving

The Maldives is one of the best diving regions in the world. Most visitors who come to the country are on an underwater pilgrimage. The variety of marine life is extensive and visibility is best during the high season from September to May.

Diving charges compare to those in the USA, which is high if you are on a budget, so try and get the diving costs included in your holiday package.

Charges, with all equipment provided, range from around US$25 to US$30 for one dive, or from US$150 to US$200 per week. It can be cheaper if you bring your own mask, snorkel and fins.

Many resorts hire out underwater photography equipment as well as all the basic gear. If you're not staying at a resort and don't have your own flippers etc, you can buy them from Shabim Emporium, near the post office on Marine Drive.

Resorts which are recommended for diving are Helengeli, Vaadu, Bandos, Kanifinolhu, Alimatha, Furana and Lankanfinolhi. Details of scuba costs, courses, sites etc are given in the info on the relevant resorts.

Kela was the northern British base during WW II, mirroring Gan at the other end of the archipelago. The mosque here dates back to the end of the 17th century. Yams and *cadjan* (mats made of coconut palm leaves) are the island's products.

Atoll to Atoll

HAA ALIF
North Tiladummati Atoll (A)
280 km from Male, 16 inhabited islands, 23 uninhabited islands, 0 resorts, population 9891.

Almost 2000 people live on Diddu, the capital island, which also offers good anchorage for passing yachts. Huvarafushi, the next largest island, is noted for its music, dancing and sporting activities and would appear to be the more interesting community. It has a fish-freezing plant.

Utheem (Utimu) is the birthplace of Mohammed Thakurufaan, the sultan who threw out the Portuguese in 1573. A memorial centre to this Maldivian hero was opened in 1986. It has a small museum. Bamboo is grown on Utheem to make fishing rods.

HAA DHAAL
South Tiladummati Atoll (B)
240 km from Male, 17 inhabited islands, 16 uninhabited islands, 0 resorts, population 11,000.

Nolivaranfaru is the capital but Kuludufushi is the main island with more than 3500 people, electricity, a community school and a hospital. The islanders have a reputation throughout the country for being hard workers. They specialise in rope making and shark fishing.

Faridu Island, at the heady elevation of three metres above sea level, is the highest point in the Maldives. It is difficult to land on.

An interesting attraction of Haa Dhaal, particularly for divers, is that because the area has suffered several severe storms this atoll is a graveyard for ships. Quite a few vessels have gone down in these waters over the years, particularly around

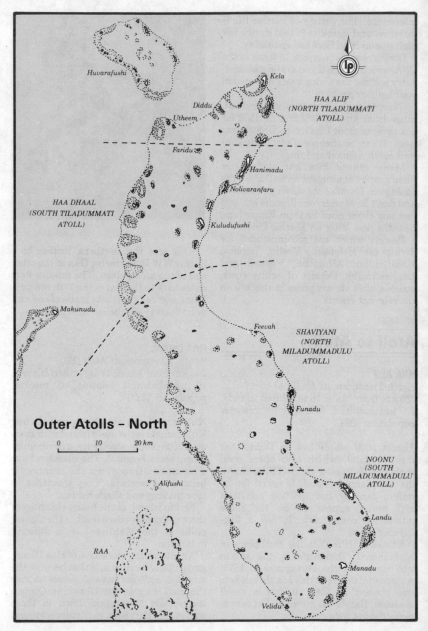

Huvarafushi

Kela

Diddu

Utheem

HAA ALIF
(NORTH TILADUMMATI
ATOLL)

Faridu

Hanimadu

Nolivaranfaru

HAA DHAAL
(SOUTH TILADUMMATI
ATOLL)

Kuludufushi

Makunudu

Feevah

SHAVIYANI
(NORTH
MILADUMMADULU
ATOLL)

Funadu

Outer Atolls – North

0   10   20 km

NOONU
(SOUTH
MILADUMMADULU
ATOLL)

Alifushi

Landu

RAA

Manadu

Velidu

the tip of Makunudu on the western side where there are three English shipwrecks as well as the *Persia Merchant* wrecked in 1658.

SHAVIYANI
North Miladummadulu Atoll (C)
192 km from Male, 15 inhabited islands, 26 uninhabited islands, 0 resorts, population 7800.

The ruins of an ancient mosque and 13th century tombstones lie on the pretty capital island of Funadu. The most populous island with almost 1000 inhabitants is Maakandudu which specialises in the production of jaggery, which is the coarse brown sugar made from date palm sap. This island has been ravaged by storms and diseases throughout history which may have something to do with why another island is called Feevah!

Naradu, with its inland lakes, is said to be the most beautiful island.

NOONU
South Miladummadulu Atoll (D)
150 km from Male, 14 inhabited islands, 57 uninhabited islands, 0 resorts, population 7000.

Manadu is the chief island but Holudu and Velidu islands are the busiest. The main attraction for any visitor would be the relic on Landu supposedly left by the fabled Redin people who are part of Maldivian folklore and magic. It is a 15-metre-high mound known locally as *maa badhige* 'great cooking pot'. Thor Heyerdahl writes extensively about the tall, fair-haired Redin in his book *The Maldive Mystery*. He believes them to have been the first inhabitants of the Maldives as long ago as 2000 BC.

RAA
North Malosmadulu Atoll (E)
145 km from Male, 16 inhabited islands, 65 uninhabited islands, 0 resorts, population 9600.

Ugufaru is the capital of this atoll which has the highest percentage of fishermen among its population of any of the atolls. The island of Alifushi is where the best dhonis in the Indian Ocean are built, even if the builders now often use wood imported from Bangladesh. The islanders also supply crafts to every atoll.

Kandoludu is the main island and said to be overcrowded with almost 2000 people. Inguraidu and Innamadu are also boatbuilding and carpentry centres. The Arab seafarer Ibn Battuta, an important figure in Maldivian history, visited Kinolhas in 1343.

BAA
South Malosmadulu Atoll (F)
105 km from Male, 13 inhabited islands, 51 uninhabited islands, 1 resort, population 7000.

Baa is famous for its lacquer work, woven cotton *felis* (the traditional sarong) and political or criminal exiles. Eydafushi, the capital and principal island, is also the feli centre. Tuladu is the second largest island, while Tulusdu and Fehendu are tops in lacquer work boxes and jars.

Fuladu Island has had two famous, or rather infamous, foreign residents. In 1602 François Pyrard, the French explorer, found himself a castaway on the island after his ship the *Corbin* was wrecked. Albert Gray, a colleague of H C P Bell, wrote about Pyrard's voyages. (A signed copy of the book is in the MID Library in Male.)

In 1976 a German traveller was banished for life to the island after he was convicted of murdering his girlfriend in a Male guest house. He is now married with two children. (The US magazine *New Look* carried a feature on him in the April 1986 edition.)

Fuladu and its neighbours, Goidu and Fehendu, have also been open prisons for many other exiles since 1962.

Hassan Ahmed Maniku noted in his book (or rather catalogue) *The Islands of*

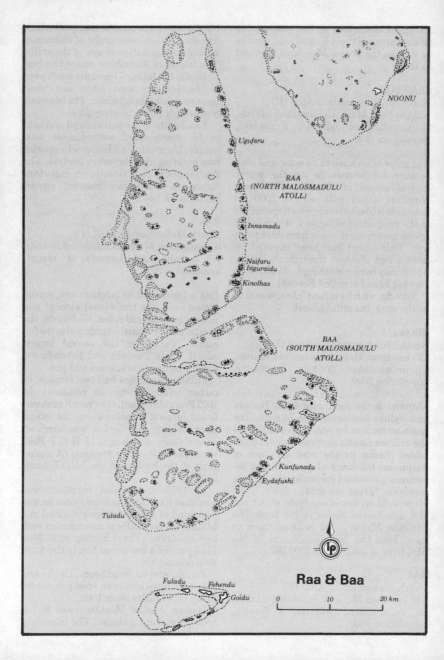

NOONU

Ugufaru

**RAA
(NORTH MALOSMADULU
ATOLL)**

Innamadu

Naifaru
Inguraidu

Kinolhas

**BAA
(SOUTH MALOSMADULU
ATOLL)**

Kunfunadu

Eydafushi

Tuladu

Fuladu   Fehendu
Goidu

Raa & Baa

0   10   20 km

the Maldives that in February 1963 more than 3.8 million flying fish 'landed' on Goidu, the separate atoll in the south (also known as Horsburgh). Whether they landed by themselves or with the help of fishermen's nets, he does not say. Maniku also said of the island: 'There is a heap of gravel and sand in almost the centre of the island measuring 41 feet in circumference and three feet high, which has never been investigated.' Heyerdahl wasn't able to oblige.

Resorts
Kunfanadu is a 50 cottage resort in the medium-price range 100 km from the airport. They offer all activities except dhoni sailing, water-skiing and tennis. The contact address in Male is Bunny Holding Pvt Ltd, Shonaree 1st floor, 29 Marine Drive. Return airport transfer is US$70.

LAVIYANI
Fadippolu Atoll (G)
120 km from Male, 4 inhabited islands, 53 uninhabited islands, 1 resort, population 6500.

All four islands are relatively crowded. Naifaru, the capital, has a reputation for concocting local medicines and making handicrafts from coral and mother-of-pearl. Hinnavaru is the next busiest island. Generally the atoll is a strong fishing centre, with a tuna cannery on Felivaru. A fish processing plant was opened in November 1986.

Resorts
Kuredu Island Resort (tel 342237) is 130 km from Hulhule Airport which makes it the most remote of the resorts. It was established in 1976 as a base for divers so the accommodation was rough and secondary to the sport. Known then as Kuredu Camping Resort it was the cheapest resort in the islands. It has since been enlarged, to 130 rooms, and

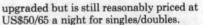
Laviyani

upgraded but is still reasonably priced at US$50/65 a night for singles/doubles.

Kuredu Island is comparatively large by Maldivian standards and used to be very popular with the West Germans. It is also known as a good base for big-game fishing.

KAAFU
North Male & South Male Atolls (H)
9 inhabited islands, 72 uninhabited islands, 35 resorts, population 8700.

North Male and South Male, the twin atolls of Kaafu, cover over 100 km of ocean from north to south and are made up of countless sandbanks and islands of which only 10 are inhabited. Male, the capital island of the Maldives, is in the south of North Male Atoll but does not come under the atoll administration.

The atoll capital, also in North Male Atoll, is the island of Thulusdu. Kaafu also includes the island atoll of Kashidu, the most populated island, to the north in the Five Degree Channel. The islanders there are big toddy tappers.

Maafushi (in South Male Atoll) has a

big children's reformatory, which opened in 1979, where the nation's delinquents undergo skill training and rehabilitation. Until 1964 the British Governor had his residence on Dhoonidhoo, just north of Male. His house is now used for prominent political prisoners.

The oil tanks you can see from Male are on Funadu Island. Also close to Male is the Kuda Bandos reserve which was saved from resort development by the government so people could enjoy it in its natural state. You do not need a permit to visit.

North Male Resorts

Helengeli (tel 344615) is 51 km from the airport and is in the low price range. It's operated by H Zonaria (tel 323339) Marine Drive, Male, is the most northerly of the Kaafu resorts and singles/doubles cost US$38/44. Helengeli is a smallish resort with a 60-bed capacity and saltwater showers. Ibrahim Rasheed, who runs the Sunshine Guest House in Male, will organise a diving or fishing holiday here at a reasonable cost.

Scuba charges on the resort are around US$175 for unlimited dives. The island has a good reef so you need not venture far for some good diving.

Eriyadu (tel 344487) is 38 km from the airport (almost three hours by boat) and, probably because of the distance, is one of the cheaper resorts. It is operated by AAA & Trading Co (tel 322417) 29 Chandani Magu, Male and singles/doubles cost US$37/51. This large, 192 bed resort is surrounded by a wide beach with plenty of trees. The diving, done with Swiss Sub-Aqua, is also good.

Makunudhoo (tel 343064), 35 km from the airport, is a medium range resort operated from PO Box 2047, Male (tel 324743). Singles/doubles cost US$75/140 and the resort, which opened in 1983, has 58 beds. It is popular with passing yachties because of the good anchorage.

Ziyaaraifushi (tel 343088) which is operated by Phoenix Travels (tel 323587) Fasmeeru, Marine Drive, Male is a medium range resort 35 km (2¼ hours by boat) from the airport. Singles/doubles cost US$25/45 and the resort recently doubled in size to 65 rooms.

Reethi Rah, or *Medhufinolhu*, (tel 342077) is 33 km from the airport next to Ziyaaraifushi. The operators are at 29 Marine Drive, Male (tel 322726) and the resort is managed by Kuoni. Singles/doubles are US$57/94. Reethi Rah means 'beautiful island'. Bungalows are in blocks of four units (motel-style) with cold water showers. The Mistral School of Windsurfers operates here and the resort is the Eurodivers diving base.

Hembadu (tel 343884), a low range resort 31 km from the airport, is operated by Journey World (tel 322016) 61 Marine Drive, Male. Singles/doubles are US$40/45 and the resort has about 30 bungalows. (Don't confuse it with Embudu.)

Asdu (tel 345051) is a medium range resort 37 km from the airport. It's operated from the Nasandhura Palace Hotel (tel 323380) Marine Drive, Male. Singles/doubles cost US$50/75. It's a small resort, with 50 beds, and offers sightseeing trips to a local fishing village on Dhiffushi.

Meerufenfushi (tel 343157) is a medium range resort, 40 km from the airport, operated by KUM (tel 322430) No 5 Ahmadhee Bazaar, Male. Singles/doubles cost US$40/55.

For some strange reason Meeru is known locally as Sweetwater Island. Tourists certainly won't find the unheated bore water gushing forth from the resort's showers all that sweet. Meeru is Kaafu's most eastern island and, covering 28 hectares, is one of the country's largest. The resort, with 174 beds, is one of the biggest and boasts a large lagoon which attracts sailboard enthusiasts.

Boduhithi (tel 343193) is in the higher price range. It's 29 km from the airport and is operated by Safari Tours (tel 323524) Chandani Magu, Male. Singles/doubles cost US$85/100. There are 66 cabanas, with freshwater showers,

Kaafu

0   10   20 km

Kashidu

Gaafuru

Olaheli

(NORTH MALE ATOLL)

Akiri-Fushi

Helengeli

Eriyadu

Boduhgli
Kudahali
Raaluara-Giri
Olu-Giri

Ziyaarai-fushi

Makunudhoo

Kuda-badhi

Reethi Rah

Hembadu

Asdu

Boduhithi

Meerufenfushi

Kudahithi

Dhiffushi

Rasfaree

Gasfinolhu

Lhohifushi

Thulusdu

Nakatchafushi

Kanifinolhu

Vabinfaru

Little Hura

Ihuru

Kanuhura

Bandos

Hima-Fushi
Lakanfushi
Lankanfinolhi

Baros

Kurumba

Furana

Kudav-atteauru

Farukolufushi

Dhoonidhoo

Hulhule

Giravaru

Villingili

Male

Velassaru

Vaadu

Embudu Finolhu

Bolifushi

Embudu

Maniyafushi

(SOUTH MALE ATOLL)

Dhigufinolhu

Waagali

Villivaru

Maafushi

Guraidhoo

Biyadoo

Ranalhi

Kandodmafushi
Losfushi

Fihal-hohi

Maadhoo

Kudafinolu

Bodufinolhu

Oaidhuni

Olhuveli

Rihiveli

surrounding the island and the resort caters mainly for Italian tourists.

Kudahithi (tel 344613) also operated by Safari Tours is a small and luxurious high range resort 28 km from the airport. A double in the high and low season is US$250. Kudahithi is one of the most exclusive islands with only six cottages, one of which is called the Sheik's Room and has a huge bath where you can do your own diving. The others are titled the King, the Rehendi (queen), Captain's Cabin, Safari Lodge and Maldivian Apartment. There's no diving here but you can go across to Boduhithi.

Nakatchafushi (tel 342665), in the upper-medium price range, is 22 km (1½ hours by dhoni) from the airport. It's operated by Universal Enterprises Ltd (tel 322971) 38 Orchid Magu, Male. Singles/doubles cost US$65/71. This 94 bed resort has individual round bures each with air-con and hot, freshwater showers. One of the most attractive features is the terrace bar over the water.

The diving school is run by West Germans. Six days of unlimited diving costs US$200 with all equipment supplied or US$160 if you bring your own gear. Six dives (with equipment provided) costs US$110 and a single dive costs US$22. There's an extra charge of US$10 per person for each boat trip.

The hiring rates for sailboards, boats and instruction are relatively high at Nakatchafushi. It's US$12 an hour to windsurf and US$22 for a lesson. Top cat catamarans cost US$18 and hour and US$30 for a lesson.

Veligandu Hura (tel 343882), also called *Palm Tree Island*, is a relatively new high range resort 53 km from the airport. It's operated by Universal Enterprises (tel 322971) 38 Orchid Magu, Male. Singles/doubles cost US$115/165 per night and there are 55 rooms.

Gasfinolhu (tel 342078), a medium range resort 18 km from the airport, is operated by Dhirham Travels & Chandling (tel 323369) Faamudheyri Magu, Male. Gasfinolhu, which means 'tree on a sandbank' is an exclusive resort with 20 cabanas.

Lhohifushi (tel 343451), in the low medium range, is 17½ km from the airport. It's operated by Altaf Enterprises (tel 323378) 8 Ibrahim Hassan Didi Magu, Male. It has about 50 units and singles/doubles cost US$40/55. The rooms are more basic than most, with ceiling fans and unheated island water. A few rooms have air-con but this costs an extra US$25 a night.

Kanifinolhu (tel 343152), 16 km from the airport, has been upgraded to a high range resort but it doesn't have a great reputation. It's operated by Cyprea (tel 322451) 25 Marine Drive, Male. Singles/doubles cost US$100/110. It's a popular resort for the younger crowd and has 106 rooms, some with air-con and all with desalinated water.

Eurodivers, led by a Spaniard, is in charge of sub-aqua on Kani. A one-week scuba course of nine dives costs US$195, plus US$45 if you go for a PADI certificate. Snorkelling is good at the southern tip of the island.

Little Hura (tel 344231), a medium range resort 16 km from the airport, is operated by the Hotel Alia (tel 322935) Male. Singles/doubles cost US$37/63 and the 38 cottages are built across the centre of the island so visitors have a choice of two beaches. You can also walk across to the local island known as Hura. The name comes from the Huraa dynasty of sultans founded in 1759 by Sultan Al-Ghaazi Hassan Izzaddeen who built a mosque there.

Leisure Island or *Kanuhura* (tel 342881), a medium range resort 15 km from the airport, is operated by Treasure Island Enterprises (tel 322165) 8 Marine Drive, Male. Also known as Tari, it has 10 cottages and singles/doubles cost US$69/86. There's no beach but the resort tries to make up for this with top restaurants, discos, tennis courts and intimacy. It's an up-market place mostly visited by Italians.

Thulhagiri (tel 342816) is 11 km from the airport. It is a totally French resort operated by Club Med which also runs the bigger and better known Farukolufushi next to Male. The agent in Male is Olympia (tel 322337) 1st floor, Ahmadhee Bazaar. Singles/doubles in the high and low season are US$80/120.

Farukolufushi (tel 343021) is the second largest resort in the Maldives, with a capacity for 304 visitors, but it doesn't offer water-skiing or tennis. You can recognise the island by the restaurant's huge and sweeping thatched roof which looks like a traditional Sulawesian house. The Club Med islands do not allow day visitors or overnight stays, and one week on Farukolufushi will set you back around US$600. They say it's where 'the best things in life are free'.

Ihuru resort was closed for renovations at the time of writing. The island is said to be the most photographed in the Maldives. The house reef, known as 'The Wall' is a handy diving spot.

Vabinfaru (tel 343147), an upper-medium range resort 16 km from the airport next to Ihuru, is operated by Dhirham Travels & Chandling (tel 323369) Faamudheyri Magu, Male. Singles/doubles cost US$60/120 in the low season and double that in the high season. This small 50 bed resort is under French management and the guests are mostly Italian and Australian. The accommodation is in thatch-roofed, round bungalows which have bore water. The food is good and some of the sports and entertainment are free.

You can take excursions to the neighbouring islands of Hima-Fushi, Thulhagiri, Boduhithi and Giravaru for US$10 per person. Windsurfing, catamaran and water skiing lessons range from US$18 to US$30. One scuba dive costs US$30, including boat, or US$160 for a certificate course.

Huduveli (tel 343396) is a medium

range resort 9½ km (50 minutes by boat) from the airport. It's operated by H Jazeera (tel 322844) Marine Drive, Male and singles/doubles cost US$46/63. Hudhuveli means 'white sand'. There are 40 bungalows built along the centre of the island each with freshwater showers. You can make arrangements to visit a local fishing village on Himmafushi. If you're visiting the resort a 'plain' meal will cost about US$15.

Lankanfinolhi (tel 343597) is a medium range, 50 cottage resort nine km from the airport. It's operated from 31 Chandani Magu, Male (tel 323186) and singles/doubles cost US$62/72.

Baros (tel 342672), a medium range resort 15 km (one hour by boat) from the airport, is operated by Universal Enterprises Ltd (tel 322971) 38 Orchid Magu, Male. Singles/doubles cost US$50/56. Baros, which is popular with UK visitors, is one of the oldest resorts and has been operating since 1973. It is half-moon shaped and has 50 bungalows, of which about half have air-con. Sub Aqua Reisen of Munich runs the diving school. The *Turtle Restaurant* is named after the little turtles found in the stream which flows around it.

Bandos (tel 343310), in the medium to high range, is eight km from the airport and is operated by Bandos Male Office (tel 322844), H Jazeera, Marine Drive, Male. Singles/doubles cost US$65/90. It was the divers on Bandos, which is the diving capital of the islands, who started feeding the sharks mouth to mouth giving rise to the tourism industry motto: 'where even the sharks are friendly'.

This large 226 bed resort has been upgraded and there are plans to make it bigger. There's a 24 hour coffee shop (meals cost around US$12), an aquarium and, nearby, the uninhabited, unspoiled island of Kuda Bandos which has been turned into a public reserve. Bandos has a decompression chamber.

Furana (tel 343878), a medium range resort 3½ km from the airport, is operated by Treasure Island Enterprises (tel 322165) 8 Marine Drive, Male. Singles/doubles cost US$49/64. Ms Janelle Reid, the Australian landlady of Furana, has the lease on the 600 metre by 200 metre island until 1990. There are 88 rooms including 10 luxury and 38 standard rooms with ceiling fans, 16 rooms with air-con, and 24 'honeymoon bungalows with garden showers'. The water is desalinated.

You can get a free ride to Furana from Male each Monday, Wednesday and Saturday at 4.30 pm on the supply dhoni. It leaves Furana at 2 pm. Furana used to sport the only casino in the Maldives.

For divers Furana is a handy base for exploring the wreck of the *Maldives Victory*, a government cargo ship which sank off Hulhule on 13 February 1981. There are other good reefs and caves nearby and the channel separating Furana from Lankanfinolhi is the haunt of whale sharks.

Giravaru (tel 344203), an upper range resort 11 km from the airport, is operated by Phoenix Travels (tel 323587) Fasmeeru, Marine Drive, Male. Singles/doubles cost US$90/130 and the facilities and 50 bungalows have been given a facelift. The bungalows have hot water and there is a freshwater swimming pool. The pool may suggest that the reef is too shallow for a proper swim.

Kurumba (tel 343084), a high range resort three km from the airport, is operated by Universal Enterprises Ltd (tel 322971) 38 Orchid Magu, Male. Singles/doubles cost US$90/100.

Kurumba, which means 'young coconut', was the first resort in the Maldives. It has

been continually expanded since it was built in 1972, including extensive renovations in 1987. It is the first of the Maldives' resorts to be classed as an international hotel which means the rooms now have all the mod cons (except TV). There are 160 rooms in thatched or tiled bungalows around the perimeter of the island, as well as a 24 hour coffee shop, a nightclub, two bars, a freshwater swimming pool, a conference and banquet hall (for up to 500 people), and a games centre which has a gymnasium and another pool.

Because it is close to Male there is more live entertainment than on other resorts, more day trippers and more visits by government and business people.

The Kurumba dive centre charges US$282 for 14 dives with tanks and weights supplied; or US$194 for six days unlimited diving.

South Male Resorts

Vaadu (tel 343976) is a high range resort eight km from the airport. It's operated by H Henveyruge, Meduziyaraiy Magu, Male and is frequented solely by Japanese. Singles/doubles cost US$80/100.

It is dubbed 'Vaadu Diving Paradise' because the island is on the edge of the deep channel which separates North and South Male atolls. It offers a great range of marine life and is arguably the best diving location in the Maldives, the only problem is that Japanese divers have exclusive rights to this resort base. Plans to establish a performing dolphins park have been considered; let's hope it doesn't go any further than that. The 33 cabanas have fresh water.

Velassaru (tel 343041), a medium range 90 bed resort 10 km from the airport, is operated by H Astoria (tel 322990) Ameer Ahmed Magu, Male. Singles/doubles are US$50/60. Built back in 1974, Velassaru officially became one of the top 300 hotels in the world until it went downhill. It's only now starting to pick up again. There

are coral walls built as windbreaks among the cottages.

Embudu Finolhu (tel 344451) is a medium range resort eight km from the airport. It's operated by Shamrock Garage (tel 324445) Chabeylee Magu, Male and is leased by an Australian. There are two classes of accommodation, basic and deluxe, and singles/doubles are US$45/60. The resort has freshwater showers and 24 of the 40 bedrooms have air-con.

A diving package of two dives each day for a week costs US$150 with tanks and weight belts provided. A single dive costs US$25 with all equipment supplied. There is an extra charge of US$6 for the boat trip and there is a range of diving courses.

Island hopping from Embudu Finolhu costs US$20 per person for a full day; while a half day trip to Male costs US$15. Windsurfing costs US$4 an hour or US$20 a day and catamaran hire is US$10 per hour.

Embudu Village (tel 342673), a medium range resort eight km from the airport, is operated by Roanuge (tel 322212) Henveiru, Ameer Ahmed Magu, Male. Singles/doubles are US$60/75 and they have hot water. It's a much bigger resort than Embudu Finolhu and has excellent snorkelling.

Bolifushi (tel 343517) is a medium range resort 13 km from the airport. It's operated by Phoenix Travels (tel 325309) Fasmeeru, Marine Drive, Male. Singles/doubles cost US$65/76 and the 32 chalets have fresh water and air-con.

Dhigufinolhu (tel 343599), a high range resort 19 km from the airport, is operated by Universal Enterprises Ltd (tel 322971) 38 Orchid Magu, Male. Singles/doubles cost US$95/125 and there are 30 rooms with open-air toilets!

Biyadoo (tel 343742) is a high range resort 28 km (2½ hours by boat) from the airport. It's operated by the Taj group through Prabalaji Enterprises (tel 322717), H Maagala, 2 Ameer Ahmed Magu, Male. Singles/doubles cost US$110/120.

Biyadoo is one of the few two-storey resorts in the Maldives. The 96 air-con rooms also have hot and cold water which, one brochure assures, is 'usually fresh'. Fresh vegetables are said to be supplied from a hydroponic garden. There is much coming and going between here and Biyadoo's next door neighbour, Villivaru resort.

There are excellent snorkelling and diving sites around the island and facilities include a Dräger decompression chamber. The Nautico watersport centre serves both Biyadoo and Villivaru. One dive, with full equipment, costs US$30 and a 10 dive package costs US$290. The PADI basic open water course is US$300 and there is a range of advanced and specialised courses.

At Biyadoo and Villivaru you can also water-ski for US$16 per three-minute round, parasail for US$30 a flight and windsurf for S$9 an hour. A catamaran will set you back US$14 an hour and a glass-bottom rowing board costs US$6 an hour.

Villivaru (tel 343598), also operated by the Taj Group, is a medium-high range resort 29 km from the airport. Singles/doubles cost US$95/120. Villivaru is the smaller sister resort of Biyadoo.

Cocoa Island (tel 343713) is a very high range resort 28 km from the airport. It's own by an ex-Playboy photographer and is operated from Chabeylee Maafannu Magu, Male (tel 322494). Doubles, in two-storey chalets with thatched roofs, cost US$172/216 in the low/high season.

Maakunufushi is the traditional name of Cocoa Island which, with only about eight chalets, is one of the exclusive retreats. Often the whole resort is rented out by one group. It's a real hedonist's hideaway.

Kanduma (tel 344452) is a low to medium range resort 31 km from the airport. It's operated by M Shana (tel 323360) 2/46 Orchid Magu, Male. Singles/doubles cost US$35/50 in the low season and only a little more in the high season. Kanduma opened in 1085 and has about 50 rooms. Visits to the nearby island of Guraidhoo can be arranged.

Bodufinolhu, or Fun Island Resort, (tel 344558) is an upgraded high range resort 38 km from the airport. It is operated from the Villa Building (tel 324478) Ibrahimee Hassan Manik Didi Magu, Male. There are 88 rooms squeezed onto this tiny island which measures only 30 by 800 metres. If it feels a little crowded there are two smaller, uninhabited islands nearby that you can walk to at low tide.

There is a nice wooden terrace bar over the lagoon and the rooms all have air-con and hot and cold desalinated water. Singles/doubles range from US$70/80 to US$90/100 throughout the year.

The resort's scuba centre charges US$25 for one dive, and US$150 for seven days of unlimited diving with equipment provided. There is an extra US$6 charge for each boat trip.

Other watersports rates are: water skiing – US$25 for 10 minutes; catamaran hire – US$20 per hour or US$75 per day; windsurfing – US$12 an hour or US$140 a week; snorkelling US$5 a day; parasailing – US$45 for 10 minutes; fishing – US$8 each, including boat and tackle, for a minimum of eight people; and island hopping – US$13 per person for half a day. An excursion to Male costs US$20.

Ranalhi (tel 342688), a medium range resort 40 km (3½ hours by boat) from the airport, is operated by Jetan Travel Services (tel 323323) 55 Marine Drive, Male. Singles/doubles cost US$45/56. Also called Rennali, the resort has 50 fan-cooled bungalows with cold, coral bore water in the showers, and five bungalows with air-con and hot water.

Fihalhohi (tel 342903), 42 km from the airport, is operated by Dhirham Travels & Chandling (tel 323372) Faamudheyri Magu, Male. There are 76 rooms and singles/doubles range from US$30/40 to US$45/55.

Olhuveli (tel 342788), 39 km from the airport, is operated by Southern Enterprises (tel 322068) 3/42 Orchid Magu, Male. Singles/doubles are US$38/50. You can only swim on one side of this island as there is a bad current on the other. When the tide is low you can walk or swim over to an adjoining island. Olhuveli, which is a very basic resort popular with Swedish tourists, has 50 rooms with saltwater showers, and the food is apparently good. It may be closed for renovations.

Rihiveli (tel 343731) is a high range resort 40 km from the airport. It's operated from Dhaharaage No 1, Chandani Magu, Male (tel 323767), is French-managed and is popular with Australians. Singles/doubles cost US$127/147.

Rihiveli, which means 'silver sand', is the southernmost resort in Kaafu. It has 39 bungalows or bures and an open-air dining room built out over the lagoon. You can wade across to the uninhabited Rising Sun island and the Island of Birds. Free snorkelling, windsurfing, water-skiing, and catamaran and dhoni sailing are part of the package. There are also free two-day cruises around the atoll on yacht-style *shada* boats, which carry four people. Eurodivers run the diving school.

ALIF
Ari Atoll (I)
64 km from Male, 18 inhabited islands, 58 uninhabited islands, 8 resorts, population 7800.

Alif includes Rasdu and Toddu the two small atolls to the north of Ari Atoll. You may think that Toddu has something to do with toddy but in fact the atoll grows watermelons. The capital and fishing centre of Alif is Mahibadu, and the islands of Mammigili and Fenfushi are the coral stone quarries of the country. Fenfushi supplies much of the sand for building in Male and is noted for its coral carvings.

More and more uninhabited islands have been allowed resort leases as the government opens up Alif for tourism. Transfer journeys from the airport to these resorts are rougher since you have to cross 40 km of open sea but the craft are high-speed ferries, not motorised dhonis.

Resorts (from north to south)
Veligandu (tel 344309) is a medium range resort on Rasdu Atoll 57 km from the airport. It is operated by Crown Tours (tel 322432) Orchid Magu, PO Box 2034, Male. Singles/doubles are US$55/80. Opened in 1985 Veligandu has 50 air-con rooms some with open-air toilets!

Kuramathi (tel 342456), a low range resort on Rasdu 55 km from the airport, is operated by Universal Enterprises (tel 323080) 38 Orchid Magu, Male. Singles/doubles cost US$35/45. The island was 'inhabited' up until 1970, but Kuramathi is now one of the largest resorts in the Maldives.

Like Baros, Kuramathi's coral reef is close to the island on one side, making it good for snorkelling, and distant on the other to allow for windsurfing and swimming. In 1868 the *Reindeer*, sailing from Mauritius, was wrecked on the reef here.

Nika Hotel (tel 344616), an 'ultimate' range resort 69 km from the airport, is

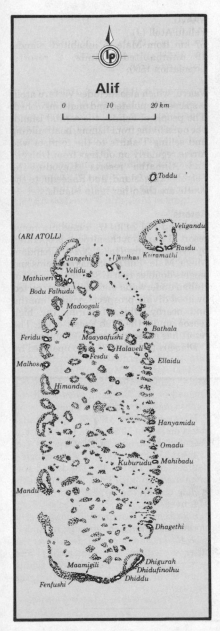

Alif

0   10   20 km

Toddu

(ARI ATOLL)

Veligandu

Gangehi
Velidu
Mathiveri
Bodu Falhudu
Madoogali

Rasdu
Ubulhaa Kuramathi

Feridu
Maayaafushi
Halaveli
Fesdu
Malhos
Himandu

Bathala

Ellaidu

Hanyamidu

Omadu
Kuburudu Mahibadu

Mandu

Dhagethi

Maamigili
Fenfushi

Dhigurah
Dhidufinolhu
Dhiddu

operated by Fantasy Trade & Travels (tel 325087) 10 Faridi Magu, PO Box 2076, Male. With prices in the US$200 to US$300 range it is supposed to be the most expensive resort in the Maldives. Nika has 16 luxurious bungalows and the island is surrounded by jetties where you can park your yacht! The Italians conceived the place, manage it and probably patronise it as well.

There was a rumour that the prices were being brought down to the US$130/140 for singles/doubles bracket, to attract more customers, but if you still can't afford it you could nip into the Gelato Italiano in Male and feel their luxurious brochures instead!

Gangehi (tel 343805) is an exclusive 25 room resort 73 km from the airport. It is operated by Sea Coast (tel 323364) 30 Marine Drive, Male and singles/doubles, in the high season, cost US$132 a night.

Madugali (tel 344881) is another newish high range resort, 78 km from the airport. It is operated from 17 Orchid Magu, Male (tel 322369) and singles/doubles cost US$80/120 in the low season and US$100/140 in the high. The transfer from the airport will cost you US$100. Madugali has 35 bungalows with air-con and the water is desalinated. The island was home to 43 Maldivians until 1943 when they were transferred to Mandu Island.

Maayaafushi (tel 343979) is a medium range resort 61 km from the airport. It's operated by Treasure Island Enterprises (tel 322165) 8 Marine Drive, Male and singles/doubles cost US$49/64. This Australian-run resort, which may be under renovation, has 60 thatched rooms and is pitched towards the younger market – up to age 35. They use cold bore water for showers. You can go for a picnic on uninhabited Magala.

Bathala (tel 343114), also operated by Treasure Island Enterprises, is the sister resort to nearby Maayaafushi. It's a medium range resort 58 km (3½ hours by boat) from the airport. Singles/doubles are US$69/86 and Bathala has 36 round thatched bungalows.

Halaveli (tel 343761), an upper-medium range resort 55 km from the airport, is operated by Akiri (tel 322719) Marine Drive, Male. There are 30 thatched bungalows in this Italian-style resort and singles/doubles are US$97/113. It's a small island, only 700 metres in diameter, surrounded by white beach.

Fesdu (tel 343741) is a medium range resort, 64 km from the airport, operated by Universal Enterprises Ltd (tel 322971) 38 Orchid Magu, Male. Fesdu has 45 round thatched houses.

Ellaidu (tel 344614), a medium range resort 57 km from the airport, is operated by Safari Tours (tel 323524) Chandani Magu, Male. There are 16 bungalows and singles/doubles cost US$60/75.

Dhidufinolhu (tel 344409), also called *Ari Beach Resort*, is a high range resort 100 km from the airport. It's operated by Golden Jet Trade & Travels (tel 322338) 13 Chandani Magu, Male and costs US$105/120 for singles/doubles. The 90 rooms apparently don't have air-con or desalinated water.

VAAVU
Felidu Atoll (J)
67 km from Male, 5 inhabited islands, 19 uninhabited islands, 2 resorts, population 1500.

Vaavu, which also includes Vattaru atoll, is sparsely populated and undistinguished. The people of Felidu, the capital island, eke out a living from fishing, boatbuilding and selling T-shirts to the tourists who arrive regularly on outings from Dhiggiri and Alimatha resorts. Keyodu, the neighbouring island, and Rakeedu, to the south, are the other main islands.

Resorts
Alimatha (tel 343044), a medium range resort 61 km from the airport, is operated by Safari Tours (tel 323524) Chandani Magu, Male. The resort has 50 rooms and singles/doubles cost US$60/85. Hordes of Italian underwater enthusiasts, attracted by good diving prospects, visit Alimatha and nearby Dhiggiri during the high season, under the Club Vacanze flag. The resort has a decompression chamber.

Dhiggiri (tel 343592), also operated by

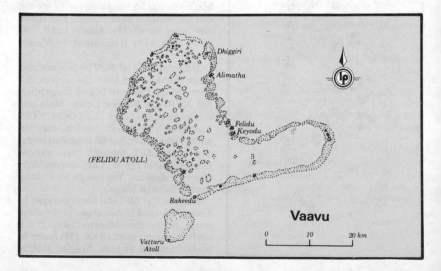

Safari Tours, is a medium range resort 59 km from the airport. Singles/doubles cost US$60/85.

MEEMU
Mulaku Atoll (K)
120 km from Male, 9 inhabited islands, 25 uninhabited islands, 0 resorts, population 3500.

Muli is the capital island but Dhiggaru, in the north of the atoll, is the most populated. Kolhufushi and Mula islands grow lots of yams.

FAAFU
North Nilandu Atoll (L)
120 km from Male, 5 inhabited islands, 10 uninhabited islands, 0 resorts, population 2300.

Thor Heyerdahl's book *Maldive Mystery* devotes an entire chapter to Faafu's central island and capital Nilandu. His expedition there unearthed five phallic lingams, and the ruins of a pre-Islamic gate which he believed to have been one of seven surrounding a great pagan temple complex.

Of Nilandu, Heyerdahl wrote:

Five teams of archaeologists could dig here for five years and still make new discoveries... the magnitude of this prehistoric cult centre seemed quite out of proportion to the size of the island.

Darabudu is famous for its turtles. They come to the island to lay their eggs during the south-west monsoon, which lasts from April to October.

DHAALU
South Nilandu Atoll (M)
150 km from Male, 8 inhabited islands, 50 uninhabited islands, 0 resorts, population 3700.

Kuda Huvadu, the capital island, is another archaeological paradise. As well as a mysterious mound, there is an old

mosque which Heyerdahl said has the finest 'fingerprint' masonry he has ever seen; surpassing, in his opinion, that of the famous Inca wall in Cuzco, Peru. He was amazed to find such a masterpiece of stone-shaping art on such an isolated island.

The waters around Kuda Huvadu also boast some shipwrecks, including the 1340 ton *Liffey* which went down in 1879.

Uninhabited Maadeli, also known as Salazar or Temple Island, has ruins which have not yet been investigated, including an ancient mosque and, according to H A Maniku, the foundations of what appears to be dwellings.

Ribudu is famous for its goldsmiths and *ras roanu* (king rope) and the island of Huludeli rivals it with a community of silversmiths.

THAA
Kolumadulu Atoll (N)
192 km from Male, 13 inhabited islands, 54 uninhabited islands, 0 resorts, population 7200.

Veimandu is the capital island of Kolumadulu which is a great circular atoll and one of the major fishing regions of the country. Thimarafushi Island, which was destroyed by fire in 1902 and again in 1905, has flourished to become the atoll's most populated island. Vilufushi Island, the next largest, has been completely overtaken by the village. There is a sultan's grave on Guraidu, which historian and archaeologist H C P Bell visited in 1922, and on Dhiyamigili there are ruins of the palace of Mohammed Imaaduddeen II, an 18th century sultan.

LAAMU
Haddummati Atoll (O)
224 km from Male, 12 inhabited islands, 75 uninhabited islands, 0 resorts, population 7300.

Laamu is a very important atoll in terms of fishing and history. The signs of pre-

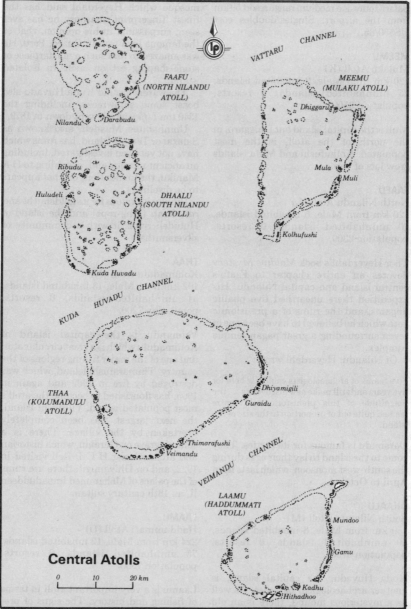

FAAFU
(NORTH NILANDU
ATOLL)

Nilandu • Darabudu

VATTARU CHANNEL

MEEMU
(MULAKU ATOLL)

Dhiggaru

Mula
Muli

Kolhufushi

Ribudu

Huludeli

DHAALU
(SOUTH NILANDU
ATOLL)

Kuda Huvadu

KUDA HUVADU CHANNEL

THAA
(KOLUMADULU
ATOLL)

Dhiyamigili
Guraidu

Thimarafushi
Veimandu

VEIMANDU CHANNEL

LAAMU
(HADDUMMATI
ATOLL)

Mundoo

Gamu

Kadhu
Hithadhoo

Central Atolls

0   10   20 km

Muslim civilisations are everywhere and include a giant black dome which rises above the palms on Isdu Island. Who built the ancient artificial mound, known as a *hawitta*, and for what reason is not really known.

Because of his research of similar structures on Gamu Island, on the eastern side of Laamu, H C P Bell believed the mounds to be the remains of Buddhist stupas, while Heyerdahl thinks maybe the Buddhists built on mounds left by the legendary Redin people. There are mounds on other islands in Laamu including Kadhu, Mundoo and the capital Hithadhoo.

One thing's for sure, if the mound on Isdu was some kind of navigational aid it proved to be of little use to several modern seafarers. The British cargo ship *Lagan Bank*, for instance, was wrecked on the reef on 13 January 1938.

An Air Maldives' Skyvan flies to Kadhu twice a week – once on the way to Gan in Seenu (Addu Atoll). Apart from the small airfield, there is nothing else on the island.

GAAF ALIF
North Huvadu Atoll (P)
330 km from Male, 10 inhabited islands, 83 uninhabited islands, 0 resorts, population 6200.

This is the northern half of the giant Huvadu, or Suvadiva, Atoll which is separated from Laamu by the 90 km wide One and a Half Degree Channel. Villingili, the capital island, is also the most populated with more than 1200 people. Devvadu islanders are famed for their textile weaving and rope making. There are also *hawittas*, the ancient mounds, on several islands in this atoll.

GAAF DHAAL
South Huvadu Atoll (Q)
360 km from Male, 10 inhabited islands, 154 uninhabited islands, 0 resorts, population 9000.

Tinadu, the capital of South Huvadu, was a focal point in the 'southern rebellion' against the central rule in Male during the early 1960s. So much so, that troops from Male invaded in February 1962 and destroyed all the homes. The people fled to neighbouring islands and Tinadu was not resettled until four years later.

Meanwhile Gaddu, which now has more than 2000 people, became the main island in the atoll. Along with the people on Fiyori, they are best known for making reed mats called *tundu kuna*. In this atoll too there is a profusion of ancient mounds most notably on the island of Gamu.

GNAVIYANI
Fuamulaku (R)
430 km from Male, 1 inhabited island, population 6300.

Fuamulaku is not really an atoll but rather a solitary island stuck in the middle of the Equatorial Channel. It is six km long, densely vegetated and surrounded by a steep, rough coral beach.

It is, however, more than just geographically different from other atolls. As a result of its geography, climate and isolation the nature of the island, and even its people, has evolved in a more exotic way than that experienced in the rest of the country. It is the only really lush island in the Maldives and produces fruits and vegetables, like mangoes, oranges and pineapples, that won't grow elsewhere.

The people look bigger and healthier than other islanders and, apparently, live longer. Thor Heyerdahl wrote: 'The people were also exceptionally beautiful and displayed far more variety in physical type than we had seen in Male'.

H C P Bell spent an eventful time on the island in 1922 investigating the ancient *hawittas*.

Fuamulaku is divided into eight districts. The main landing point is at Rasgefanu, in Malegamu district, and the island has two inland freshwater lakes,

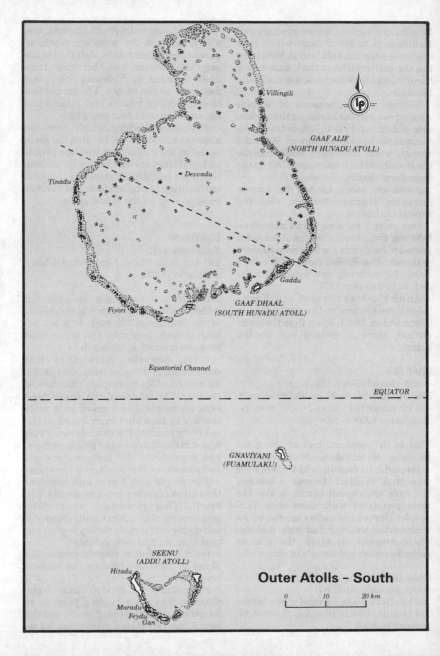

Villingili

**GAAF ALIF
(NORTH HUVADU ATOLL)**

Devvadu

Tinadu

Gaddu

Fiyori

**GAAF DHAAL
(SOUTH HUVADU ATOLL)**

Equatorial Channel

EQUATOR

**GNAVIYANI
(FUAMULAKU)**

**SEENU
(ADDU ATOLL)**

Hitadu

Maradu
Feydu
Gan

Outer Atolls – South

0   10   20 km

Bandara Kuli (or Kelhe) and Dadimage Kuli.

The one big drawback to the island is the sea and coastline. The small reef is hardly protective and the coral shingle beach drops straight down to the water. There is no safe anchorage, fishing is dangerous and swimming is suicidal because of treacherous currents. Still, Fuamulaku has a great drawing power for travellers and (with the permit and the plane from Male) can be reached easily from Addu Atoll to the south.

There are no regular sea connections across the 50 km gap between Addu and Fuamulaku. You can check the Addu Development Authority and the State Trading Organisation to see if any fast boats are making the trip, otherwise there is the occasional fishing or ferry dhoni.

SEENU
Addu Atoll (S)
478 km from Male, 7 inhabited islands, 36 uninhabited islands, 1 resort, population 15,000.
This is the 'second city' of the Maldives, after Male, and the only other atoll with traffic. The rivalry between the two cities is similar to the north-south divisions in the USA and the UK.

There is a fierce independent streak in the Addu folk, reflected in the fact that they even speak differently from the people of Male. Tensions last came to a head in the 1960s under the leadership of Abdulla Afif Didi, the elected president of the 'United Suvadiva Islands'. The shortlived southern uprising was quashed, however, by an armed fleet sent south by Prime Minister Ibrahim Nasir. Afif fled the country but is still talked about on his home island of Hitadu.

Where isolation had a big influence on Fuamulaku's character, it was the Royal Air Force which shaped the personality of Addu Atoll. The British had an air base on the island of Gan during WW II and again from 1956 to 1976.

They built a causeway connecting Feydu, Maradu and Hitadu islands, paved the roads and employed most of the population on or around the base. They left an airport, an industrial estate, a 'holiday village' and a lot of unemployed people who spoke better English than anyone in the rest of the country. When the tourist industry took off in the 1970s, many of the men of Addu went to Male to work on resorts or in stores and continued to serve the *don miha* (tourists or expats).

The only registered places to stay and eat in the Maldives, apart from the resorts, are here on Seenu - the southernmost atoll. If you are looking for someone to 'sponsor' a visit to the islands and get you a permit, chances are you'll find someone from Addu although, technically, a permit is not needed if you are staying at Gan Holiday Village.

Gan
The remains of several mosques and other earlier ruins in this region were all flattened by the 'Arif'. When the locals started showing me ruins of the subsequent Arif dwellings on Feydu Island, I at first thought the 'Arif' was another legendary tribe like the Redin. It took me a while to realise that the ruins were demolished bungalows, circa 1960s, and the 'Arif' was the RAF!

The British took over the whole of Gan and installed all the comforts of home. Now it's like a ghost town, quiet and eerie.

However, with Australian aid, the airport is being slowly modernised with the hopes of one day being able to accommodate jet-loads of tourists. At present only the 18-seater Skyvan arrives three times a week.

Hangars and other maintenance buildings have been taken over by two Hong Kong garment factories. These businesses bus in 1500 local women but also employ about 500 Sri Lankan girls, who live for a year or two in the former barracks and work nightshift without any leave.

Spring Cinema on Maradu, Addu Atoll

The cinema is still operational and there is a post office and a Bank of Maldives. Sadly the swimming pool is now more like a cesspool and the golf course is closed and so overgrown it's hard to spot the clubhouse, let alone the fairway. Pakistanis employed by the RAF, for cooking and other domestic chores, built a mosque which is still standing and, though no longer used, is more elaborate than the Maldivian one.

Gan Holiday Village, run under the auspices of the Addu Development Authority (tel 313101), is in the low to medium range for resort accommodation – which is very expensive for what you get. It's more like a 1950s British holiday camp and nothing like any of the other resorts. But it is the only official place to stay outside of Male and the other resorts.

Little has changed since the air force flew away for good in 1976. The former quarters of the officers and NCOs are now guest rooms. The bar, games room and dining room once belonged to the Sergeants' Mess; while the Officers' Mess is now reserved for visiting dignitaries.

The village is deserted most of the year and the diving school has closed temporarily. Guests can't, and wouldn't want to, swim around Gan itself but they do have good access to other islands.

Hitadu

After driving straight through Feydu and Maradu you come to Hitadu, the big capital of the atoll. A taxi from Gan airport or the Holiday Village costs between Rf 50 and Rf 60.

Hitadu is clustered around Aazee Magu, the long central avenue. Electricity is available on the island from 6 to 11 pm. There is a VSO nurse in charge of the hospital when there is no doctor posted to the island.

The best place to swim is Cortez (pronounced 'kottey') Beach at the northern point of the island where there is a break in the reef. Elsewhere the coast is too rocky or shallow for bathing. Near Cortez are the ruins of a sultan's fort.

Across the lagoon from Hitadu, on the other side of the heart-shaped atoll, are the 'siamese' islands of Huludu and Meedu. On the latter there is a revered cemetery, called Koagannu, where several important gazis are buried.

While in Hitadu, you will probably come across Hussein Ali Dhilkashge, the island's mudeem. You'll recognise him by his bike, adorned with bells and horns; and if you don't see him, you'll hear him. He is one of the country's great characters – a colourful local vicar, if you like. His religious speeches are peppered with funny anecdotes and his humour is as comforting as his advice. Hussein is the complete opposite of what you might imagine a mudeem to be like and in Hitadu he is treated like a seer.

Down by the fishing harbour there are four local cafes or tearooms, including the *Marine*.

The only place to go for a European meal is *Target Point* on Aazee Magu. Whether you are having a Coke or the chef's special spaghetti bolognaise, it is served in style by a young waiter in a white shirt and bow tie. He is obviously training for resort work when he leaves school and Hitadu.

Everyone gets around Hitadu on bicycles. Visitors will have to hire a bike privately. It is also possible to organise dhoni trips across to uninhabited islands for camping and fishing.

ISLANDS
OF THE
EAST
INDIAN
OCEAN

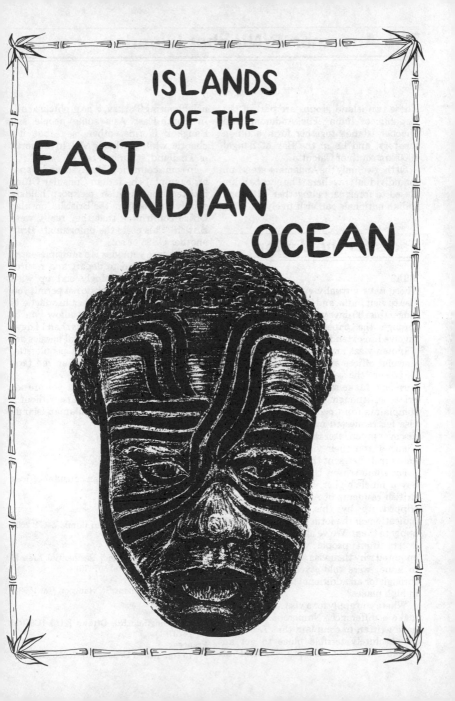

The Andaman & Nicobar Islands

These two island groups are part of the Republic of India. The Andaman and Nicobar islands together form a union territory, and lie in the Bay of Bengal 1000 km south of Calcutta.

Of the two, only the Andamans are set up for individual travellers. The Nicobars are closed to foreigners altogether, although Indian nationals can visit freely.

Facts for the Visitor

VISAS

These days virtually everybody needs a visa to visit India, and if you intend to stay longer than 90 days you will also have to go through the paperwork and red tape involved in extending a visa.

Indian visas are available from Indian consular offices and usually cost around US$5 or the equivalent in another currency. Make sure you know what the price is, though. We've had several complaints from people who sent in the visa fee requested on the form, only to discover much later that the fee had been changed and their visa request was on hold until they sent the correct amount.

For some reason UK citizens have to pay a much higher visa fee, and many British residents of Australia have been tripped up by this, as there is no indication on the form that different fees apply to them. We've also had a couple of letters from people who, when they enquired why their visa was taking so long to issue, were told it could be rushed through for an additional fee! Corruption in high places?

Where you apply for a visa also seems to make a difference. Numerous travellers have written to complain that Athens is an absolutely terrible place to get an Indian visa but Ankara, capital of neighbouring Turkey, is no problem at all. In South-East Asia some people say Bangkok is fine, others say that it's chaotic; while in Chiang Mai, in the north of Thailand, it's a breeze.

In some countries (Malaysia and Nepal for example) the Indian Consular Office insisted that British passport holders supply a letter from the British Consular Office confirming that they really were British! This costs the unfortunate Brits another US$5 or so!

Make sure your visa is a multiple-entry one if you intend to depart and return. Some people unwittingly end up with single-entry visas which do not permit you to return to India. Another headache is that some offices will not allow you to renew your visa until it is less than 14 days from expiry. The visa renewal hassles are not due to reluctance to let people stay longer, but to the usual Indian red tape and bureaucracy.

Note Even if you have a visa, you are not allowed to visit the Andamans without a special permit. See the Andaman Islands section for details.

Embassies

Some of the major Indian consular offices overseas include:

Australia
  3-5 Moonah Place, Yarralumla, ACT 2600 (tel (062) 733999)
Bangladesh
  120 Rd 2, Dhanmodi Residential Area H No 129, Dhaka (tel 507670)
Burma
  545-547 Merchant St, Rangoon (tel 15933, 16381)
Canada
  10 Springfield Rd, Ottawa K1M 1C9 (tel 7443751)
France
  15 Rue Alfred Dehodencq, 75016 Paris

Japan
 2-11 Kudan Minami 2-Chome, Chiyoda-ku, Tokyo (tel 2622391)
Malaysia
 United Asian Bank Building, 19 Malacca St, Kuala Lumpur (tel 221766)
Nepal
 Lainchaur, GPO Box 292, Kathmandu (tel 211300)
Netherlands
 Buitenrustwg 2, The Hague (tel (070) 469771)
New Zealand
 180 Molesworth St, Princess Towers, Wellington (tel 736390)
Pakistan
 482-F Sector G-6/4, Islamabad (tel 821049)
Singapore
 India House, 31 Grange Rd (tel 7376777)
Sri Lanka
 3rd floor, State Bank of India Building, 18-3/1 Sir Baron Jayatilaka Mawatha, Colombo 1 (tel 21604, 22788)
Switzerland
 Weltportstr 17, 3015 Berne (tel (031) 440193)
Thailand
 46 Soi Prasarmitr, Sukhumvit 23, Bangkok (tel 2580300)
UK
 India House, Aldwych, London WC2B 4NA (tel (01) 8368484)
USA
 2107 Massachusetts Ave NW, Washington DC 20008 (tel 9397000)
West Germany
 Adenaverallee 262, 5300 Bonn (tel 54050)

Visa Extensions

If your stay in India is going to be more than 90 days and you have to extend your visa, then you'll need to have a few days to spare while you wait for it to come through. The time taken varies from one hour (Bangalore) to 10 days (Cochin), and a lot of people have reported that they are not issuing extensions *at all* in Goa. Officially there is no charge for visa extensions, although public servants fishing for baksheesh are not unheard of. Four identical passport photos are needed.

 If you leave the country and pop across the border to Nepal after 60 days, for

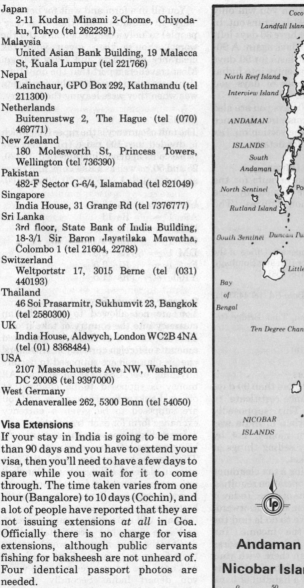
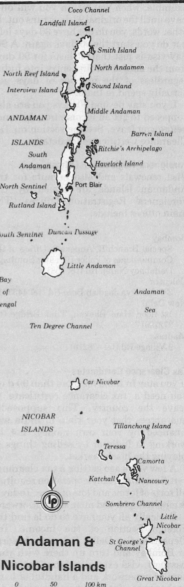

example, when you return you will only have until the original 90 days runs out. In other words, you do not have 30 days left, nor do you start the 90 days again. A 90-day visa is just that; it lasts for 90 days from the date of the first entry into India, regardless of the number of days you actually spend in India.

If you stay beyond 90 days you are also supposed to get an income tax clearance before you leave. See the section on Tax Clearance Certificates for details.

Foreigners' Registration Offices
Visa renewals and also permits for the Andaman Islands are issued by the Foreigners' Registration Offices. The main offices include:

Bombay
    Special Branch II, Annexe 2, Office of the Commissioner of Police (Greater Bombay), Dadabhoy Naroji Rd (tel 268111)
Calcutta
    237 Acharya Jagdish Bose Rd (tel 443301)
New Delhi
    1st floor, Hans Bhavan, Tilak Bridge (tel 272790)
Madras
    9 Village Rd (tel 478210)

Tax Clearance Certificates
If you stay in India for more than 90 days you need a 'tax clearance certificate' to leave the country. This supposedly guarantees that your time in India was financed by your own money, not by working in India or by selling things or playing the black market.

A few years ago getting a tax clearance certificate was a major operation requiring all sorts of forms and lots of time. Today it is much simpler and more straightforward.

Basically all you have to do is find the Foreign Section of the Income Tax Department in Delhi, Calcutta, Madras or Bombay and turn up there with your passport, visa extension form, any other similar paperwork and a handful of bank exchange receipts (to show you really did change foreign currency into rupees).

You fill in a form and wait for between 'only 10 minutes' (for the 'best-case' people) to 'only a couple of hours' (for the worst). You're then given your tax clearance certificate and away you go. Most travellers report that the only time they were asked to produce this certificate was when they were leaving the country.

MONEY
The unit of currency is the rupee (Rs) which is divided into 100 paise (p). There are paise coins in denominations of 5, 10, 20, 25 and 50, as well as a Rs 1 coin; and there are notes of Rs 1, 2, 5, 10, 20, 50 and 100.

US$ 1 =	Rs	16.5
A$ 1 =	Rs	13
UK£1 =	Rs	26.5
C$ 1 =	Rs	14
DM 1 =	Rs	8.5
Fr 1 =	Rs	2.5
Y100 =	Rs	11.5

Currency Exchange Forms
You are not allowed to bring Indian currency into the country or take it out. You are allowed to bring in unlimited amounts of foreign currency or travellers' cheques but you are supposed to declare anything over US$1000 on arrival. All money is supposed to be changed at official banks or moneychangers, and you are supposed to be given a currency exchange form for each transaction.

In actual practice you can surreptitiously bring rupees into the country with you. They can be bought at a useful discount price in places like Singapore or Bangkok and can be brought in fairly openly from Nepal, where you'll also get a slightly better rate.

Banks will usually give you a currency exchange form but occasionally they don't bother. It is, however, worth getting them for several reasons. First of all, you will need one for any re-exchange when you depart India. Secondly, certain official purchases, such as airline tickets, must be paid for either with foreign currency or with rupees accompanied by sufficient exchange forms to account for the ticket price. Thirdly, if you stay more than 90 days and have to get an income tax clearance, this requires production of a handful of exchange forms to prove you've been changing money all along and not earning money locally.

Travellers' Cheques

Due to problems of fraudulent use some banks, principally State Bank of India branches, will not accept American Express travellers' cheques. Although most of the time they are OK, it's probably wise to bring at least a few other travellers' cheques just in case.

Credit Cards

Although credit cards are widely accepted in India, their use in the Andamans is restricted to the resort hotels.

TIPPING

In tourist restaurants or hotels, where service is usually tacked on in any case, the normal 10% figure normally applies. In smaller places, where tipping is optional, you need only tip a couple of rupees, not a percentage of the bill. Hotel porters usually get about Rs 1 per bag, while Rs 1 to Rs 2 is a good level for bike watching and Rs 5 to Rs 15 is the norm for extra services from hotel staff.

TOURIST INFORMATION
Overseas Reps

The Government of India Tourist Office maintains a string of tourist offices overseas where you can get brochures, leaflets and some information about India and the Andamans. The quality of information in the tourist office leaflets and brochures is often very high and they are worth getting hold of. On the other hand, some of the overseas offices are not always as useful for obtaining information as those within India.

The overseas offices are given in the following list; there are also smaller 'promotion offices' in Osaka (Japan) and in Dallas, Miami, San Francisco and Washington DC (all USA).

Australia
   Carlton Centre, 55 Elizabeth St, Sydney NSW 2000 (tel (02) 2321600)
   8 Parliament Court, 1076 Hay St, West Perth WA 6005 (tel (09) 3216932)
Austria
   Opernring 1/F/II, 1010 Vienna (tel 5871462)
Belgium
   60 Rue Ravenstein, Boite 15, 1000 Brussels (tel (02) 5111796)
Canada
   60 Bloor St, West Suite No 1003, Toronto, Ontario M4W 3B8 (tel (416) 9623787)
France
   8 Blvd de la Madeleine, 75009 Paris 9 (tel 42658386)
Italy
   Via Albricci 9, 20122 Milan (tel 804952)
Japan
   Pearl Building, 9-18 Ginza, 7 Chome, Chuo ku, Tokyo 104 (tel 5715062/3)
Malaysia
   Wisma HLA, Lot 203 Jalan Raja Chulan, 50200 Kuala Lumpur (tel 2425301)
Singapore
   Podium Block, 4th floor, Ming Court Hotel, Tanglin Rd, Singapore 1024 (tel 2355737)
Sweden
   Sveavagen 9-11 (Box 40016), S-III-57 Stockholm (tel (08) 215081)
Switzerland
   1-3 Rue de Chantepoulet, 1201 Geneva (tel (022) 321813)
Thailand
   Singapore Airlines Building, 3rd floor, 62/5 Thaniya Rd, Bangkok (tel 2352585)
UK
   7 Cork St, London WIX QAB (tel (01) 43736778)
USA
   30 Rockefeller Plaza, 15 North Mezzanine, New York NY 10020 (tel (212) 5864901)
   230 North Michigan Ave, Chicago IL 60601 (tel (312) 2366899)
   3550 Wilshire Blvd, Suite 204, Los Angeles CA 90010 (tel (213) 3808855)
West Germany
   Kaiserstrasse 77-III, 6000 Frankfurt Main-1 (tel 235423)

Andaman Islands

Named after the monkey god, Hanuman, these islands were originally inhabited by six Negrito tribes. In recent times, however, large numbers of Indians have arrived from the mainland to settle here. Despite this the islands are still very much a backwater.

Although patience, persistence and time are all needed in large quantities, the Andamans offer some spectacular diving and snorkelling and the chance to explore rarely visited islands.

HISTORY

As the Andamans lie on the ancient trade routes between India and the Far East, they were known to mariners from as early as the 7th century, and probably long before that. Marco Polo wrote of them in the 13th century, warning of the fiercely hostile people who would kill and eat any outsider who ventured onto the islands. These reports were 'substantiated' in later centuries and the islands became synonymous with murder and brutality, although it was subsequently shown that the islanders did not practise cannibalism.

The Andaman Islands were first settled by the British in the late 18th century when Captain Archibald Blair, sailing on behalf of the British East India Company in Calcutta, founded a naval station on Chatham Island, now known as Port Blair. Attempts were then made to settle areas in the north of Great Andaman, but the hostility of the local inhabitants forced the British to abandon those plans.

In 1858 a penal colony was established in Port Blair, mainly as a solution to dealing with the large numbers of Indians held by the British following the so-called 'Indian Mutiny' of 1857. The first batch of 200 'mutineers', two doctors and 60 British naval troops arrived aboard the *Semiramis* on 10 March 1858.

These first convicts were put to work clearing extensive areas of jungle and reclaiming swampy areas. Despite the huge number of casualties from sickness and disease in the early years, the settlement gradually took shape. Because of the high mortality rate, however, the prisoners nicknamed the settlement *Kalapani* – 'water of death'.

A letter from the superintendent of the penal colony, J P Walker, to the Secretary of India in June 1858 gives the following statistics on the number of convicts that arrived on prison ships that year and their survival rate.

Received per *Semiramis* from Calcutta	10 March	200
Received per *Roman Emperor* from Kurachee	6 April	171
Received per *Edward* from Kurachee	13 April	130
Received per *Dalhousie* from Calcutta	15 April	140
Received per *Sesostris* from Singapore	12 June	132
	Total	773

Died in hospital	64
Escaped uncaptured	140
Suicide	1
Executed	87
Living	481

The islands really gained notoriety in 1872 when a visiting viceroy, Lord Mayo, was assassinated by a Muslim convict, Sher Ali.

In 1876 the British introduced the *Andaman & Nicobar Manual*, which included the following definition:

Transportation entails hard labour with strict discipline, with only such food as is necessary. Any mitigation of the above is an indulgence which may at any time be withdrawn in part or whole.

By 1881 the population had grown to 14,628, most of whom were convicts. A vast majority of the convicts, who were released after they had served their time, actually stayed and settled in the Andamans.

Following a visit by the Lyall &

Top: Islands in the sun (HM)
Bottom: Coral (PS)

Top: A beach anywhere in the Maldives (PS)
Bottom: Dhonis at sunset (HM)

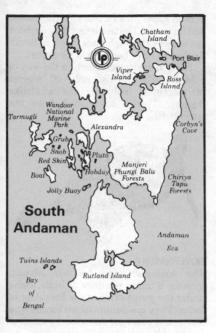

Andaman Branch of the Indian Independence League, an anti-British force formed on the mainland. Other men, women and children were said to have been taken out to sea and dumped in the water to drown.

After the war the British decided to close down the penal settlement. The decision was reported in the *Amrita Bazar Patrika* newspaper:

New Delhi, Sept 1, 1945. The Government of India has decided to abolish the penal settlement in the Andaman Islands as a major step towards their reoccupation. The reasons for its abolition are, it is pointed out, firstly political bitterness which the dispatch of prisoners to those islands created, secondly jails being a provincial subject, the centre has no needs to run the penal settlement, and thirdly communication difficulty.

When India gained independence from Britain, the islands became part of the Indian Union. The main activity since then has been the logging of the forests. The government goes to great lengths to make it known that this is all in the best interest of the tribal people, and that they are bringing civilisation to these stone-age tribes. The fact is that the tribes have been decimated by imported diseases and their cultures have been severely undermined.

In recent years the government has adopted a somewhat more responsible attitude to logging and settlement. The tribal settlements are also off limits to unauthorised visitors, so it is hoped that their culture, and indeed the tribes themselves, will survive.

GEOGRAPHY
Together with the Nicobar Islands, the Andamans are a part of a mostly submarine mountain range joining Burma and the Indonesian island of Sumatra. The 204 islands of the group cover a total of 6340 square km.

The three main islands in the group are North, Middle and South Andaman, which are known collectively as Great Andaman.

Lethbridge Commission, sent to the Andamans by the British to investigate the penal system, a decision was taken to build a jail as it was thought the conditions were too good compared with other jails on mainland India. Also there was nowhere to keep prisoners in solitary confinement, which was one of the favourite forms of incarceration at the time. Construction of Port Blair's Cellular Jail began in 1891.

During WW II the Japanese occupied the islands after the British beat a hasty retreat, taking their most prized prisoners with them to Calcutta. The Japanese established a major defence base and evidence of their presence, such as huge concrete bunkers, can still be seen today.

During the period of Japanese occupation, many Indians were arrested and tortured on suspicion of being British spies. Most were in fact members of the

Other important islands include Landfall, Interview, Ritchie's Archipelago, Baratang and Rutland. Little Andaman Island lies some 80 km south of South Andaman, and is separated from the main group by Duncan Passage.

There is a large number of small islands dotted in and around the passages which separate the islands of Great Andaman. Port Blair is the administrative capital and is situated on a sheltered harbour on the south-west coast of South Andaman. Islands in the vicinity which can be visited include Ross, Grub, Jolly Buoy, Red Skin, Snob and Boat.

The main islands are extremely hilly and are covered in dense forest (where it hasn't been cleared). The hills rise steeply, the highest being Saddle Peak (750 metres) in North Andaman. There are no permanent rivers and only a very few perennial streams.

CLIMATE
The climate of the Andamans is warm all year round, with generally high humidity, although the afternoon sea breezes temper this. Daytime temperatures average around 30°C and rarely fall below 22°C.

Most of the islands' annual rainfall of 3161 mm occurs during the south-west monsoon season from June to September, with lighter falls in May and through the months of October and November during the north-east monsoon. The wettest month is usually June with an average rainfall of 590 mm, while from January to April the averages range from three mm (in March) to 71 mm.

Despite being affected by cyclones in the Bay of Bengal, the Andamans rarely suffer any severe damage, although transport and communications links may be cut for a few days at a time.

The best time for a visit is from mid-November to April.

FLORA & FAUNA
The native Andaman redwood (*pterocarpus dalbergioides*) is exported to Europe and is used locally for building boats, houses and furniture. The tree is found throughout the islands although large tracts in South Andaman have been felled for export.

There is really not much in the way of wildlife. There exist only 20 species of mammal, including the whalelike dugong. Turtles are fished from the surrounding waters.

GOVERNMENT
The Andaman and Nicobar islands, forming a union territory of India, come under the jurisdiction of the President of India. They are administered locally by a lieutenant governor and a local council of five members.

ECONOMY
The economy of the islands is based around the timber industry, although fishing plays an important role on a local scale.

The major crops grown include rice, coconuts and areca nuts (betel nut).

POPULATION & PEOPLE
The population of the Andamans is currently around 200,000, most of whom are immigrants from the Indian mainland and Sri Lanka. These days the tribal people number only about 600, down from well over 5000 before the arrival of the British in the mid-19th century.

In the past the government's policy towards the tribal people of the Andamans leaned more heavily towards assimilation rather than protection. Former prime minister Jawaharlal Nehru, however, had the right idea:

There is no point in trying to make of them a second-rate copy of ourselves. They are a people who sing and dance and try to enjoy life; not people who sit in stock exchanges, shout at each other, and think themselves civilised. We do not mean to interfere with their way of life, but want to help them live it according to their own genius and tradition.

The tribes are of Negrito stock and inhabit only small pockets throughout the islands.

The Great Andamanese tribe once numbered 5000 but today is reduced to less than 20, and these people are all of mixed blood. They live in huts constructed by the government on tiny Strait Island off the east coast of Middle Andaman. In the early days of British settlement diseases such as malaria, syphilis, diphtheria and measles rapidly halved the tribe's numbers. The Europeans also brought with them opium, tobacco and alcohol, and these were given as reward when the tribespeople caught and turned in escaped convicts from the penal settlement.

The Onges number about 100 and live in a few small areas on Little Andaman. Their numbers have rapidly declined due to being cut off from the other Andaman tribes. Close to the Onge villages are settlements of Nicobarese and Bangladeshi refugees settled there by the government.

The Onge are small, dark-complexioned hunters and gatherers, who wear no clothes other than tassled genital decorations and who are fond of colourful make-up. Their striking facial decorations are made from an ochre paste which also gives protection from flies and mosquitoes.

The Onges still live largely off the forest, although they do barter coconuts and honey for manufactured produce, such as flour, tobacco, tea and wheat, from the government store. Dogs were introduced early this century and the Onges have domesticated them and use them for hunting the wild pigs which inhabit the islands. Dugong and turtle are also part of the Onges' diet, although these creatures are becoming quite rare.

The Jarawas were hostile to overtures from visitors right up until the 1970s, and even now only a small number have responded to attempts to 'civilise' them. The tribe numbers about 250 people and they live in reserves on the west coasts of Middle and South Andaman.

The last group, the Sentinelese, live on North Sentinel Island off the west coast of South Andaman. The 150 or so tribespeople still fiercely resist any attempts to integrate them, and live now much as they have done for centuries.

RELIGION

The religion of the Andamanese is not well documented. It is known that one tribe has a supreme god called Puluga, whose appearance is firelike but who is actually invisible. He is immortal and is angered by certain sins. The people also believe in other spirits which reside in either the forest or the sea. The sun is the wife of the moon, and the stars are their children.

LANGUAGE

The local language is Andamanese, although it is spoken by very few people these days. As is the case in mainland India, English and Hindi are the languages of popular communication. Andamanese is unusual in that, as far as can be established, it is not related to any other language.

SPECIAL PERMIT

Even with an Indian visa you are not allowed to visit the Andamans without a special permit.

If you are arriving in these islands by ship, you need a permit in advance. For air passengers permits are issued on arrival in Port Blair. The permits are also obtainable from an embassy or consulate abroad or from the Ministry of Home Affairs in New Delhi. The application to these places must be made at least six weeks in advance – in fact they recommend that you allow 12 weeks. In Madras, however, you can get a permit in just three days.

The permit is valid for a 15 day visit in the Port Blair municipal area only. To travel outside that area you need yet another permit, which is available from the District Commissioner in Port Blair. It allows visits only (overnight stays not permitted) to Jolly Buoy, Cinque, Red Skin, Grub, Snob and Boat islands – all small islands which form part of the Wandoor National Marine Park on the west coast of South Andaman.

TOURIST INFORMATION
Local Tourist Offices

There are two tourist offices in the Andamans, both in Port Blair. One is run by the local municipality, the other by the Government of India.

For more information within India, contact either the Public Relations Officer, Andaman & Nicobar Administration, F 105 Kasturba Gandhi Marg, New Delhi (tel 387015); or the Public Relations Office, Andaman & Nicobar Administration, 3-A Auckland Place, Calcutta (tel 442604).

GENERAL INFORMATION
Post

The Indian postal service is fairly efficient, although letters posted in the Andamans can take a while to arrive at their destination.

Telephone

Telephone links with the mainland are tenuous at best. It is not at all uncommon for the line to be inexplicably 'out' for hours on end. Don't come here if you need to communicate with the outside world.

Electricity

Electricity is 240 volts, 50 cycles. Unlike elsewhere in the country, there is plenty of power in Port Blair. The huge generators down near the port pump out power 24 hours a day. As it is all subsidised, hotels and restaurants here are probably the best lit in the country.

Time

As part of the central government's attempts to make the islanders feel as though they belong, the Andaman Islands run on Indian mainland time. This is despite that fact they are much closer to Burma than they are to India. The result is that it gets light at about 4 am, and darkness starts to set in around 5 pm – a crazy situation.

Film & Photography

Film should definitely be brought with you from the mainland or, preferably, from outside India. It is available locally but the quality is suspect.

Books

Leaving aside the usual histories and anthropological studies, there is a ripping colonial yarn titled *Murder in the Andamans* by M M Kaye (Penguin, London, reprinted 1986). It's a whodunit set during WW II. Ms Kaye is perhaps better known for penning *The Far Pavilions*.

Accommodation

The only hotels in the Andamans are in Port Blair. There are both private and government-run places, and these run all the way from filthy flophouses to resorts with star ratings.

GETTING THERE

Air

Indian Airlines has four flights a week between Port Blair and Madras (Rs 1255) or Calcutta (Rs 1245). The flights take two hours and are often booked up weeks in advance.

Make sure you have a confirmed seat for your flight from Port Blair to the mainland before leaving Madras or Calcutta. The reservation and waiting list system on the island is a bit of a hit-and-miss affair.

Boat

There are regular sailings between Port Blair and Madras, and Port Blair and Calcutta. The Shipping Corporation of India operates these vessels and puts out a schedule roughly every three months, so it's possible to plan fairly well in advance. Foreigners have to travel 1st or 2nd class. There are usually just monotonous *thalis* (fixed-price, set-menu meals) for breakfast, lunch and dinner so you need to bring something to supplement this boring diet.

Visitors arriving in the islands by boat need to get their permit in either Madras or Calcutta before buying the boat ticket.

In Port Blair the SCI office in the Secretariat is open for Madras bookings from 10 to 11 am and 2 to 3 pm, and for Calcutta bookings from 10 am to 12 noon and 2 to 4 pm.

The ships MV *Nejd II* and MV *Nejd III* operate a twice-weekly (usually) service between Madras and Port Blair. The journey is supposed to take about 56 hours but is often longer due to rough seas. The boats have air-con, and a daily charge of Rs 40 is made for food. The fares are Rs 583 1st class and Rs 375 2nd class.

The MV *Andamans* connects Port Blair with Calcutta, making about two journeys per month. In Port Blair bookings close four days before the scheduled departure date. The fares are Rs 583 in C class and food is charged for at the rate of Rs 38 per day.

Tours

Penthouse Tours in Sydney offer an 11 day tour to the Andamans starting from A$1798 per person, staying at the *Andaman Beach* or *Bay Island* hotels and including airfares via Bangkok and Calcutta.

GETTING AROUND

Air

The Monday flight from Calcutta goes on to Car Nicobar. The fare is Rs 325.

Indian Airlines also operates a helicopter service between Port Blair and a few of the outlying islands, and to Car Nicobar.

Fares to Car Nicobar are Rs 488, but this route is not open to foreigners.

Road

There is a small road network around South Andaman, although to travel outside the Port Blair area a permit is required from the District Commissioner. (See Permits sections.)

Buses operate from the bus station in Port Blair, although the destinations they serve are limited. It's also possible to hire taxis or bicycles for exploring.

Boat

There are boat services to other islands but foreigners need special permission to travel on them. As most of the islands are not open to foreigners anyway, these boats are of limited use.

PORT BLAIR

Port Blair is the administrative capital and only town of any size in the islands. It has the lively air of any Indian market town but lacks the crush of people, bullock carts and vehicles that usually crowd the scene. It is pleasantly situated on the main harbour and, as it's a hilly town, there are good views from quite a few vantage points.

Information & Orientation

The town is spread out over a few hills, but the main concentration of hotels, the bus station, passenger dock and Shipping Corporation of India office are in the main bazaar area, known as Aberdeen Bazaar. The airport is a few km south of town over at least one steep hill.

The Government of India Tourist Office (tel 21006) is in a crazy location, half-way between the airport and the Secretariat building, at least 20 minutes walk from the centre. They have nothing of interest anyway, so don't waste your time.

There is a local tourist office (tel 20380) at the Tourist Home at Middle Point. This is where you need to enquire about boats to other islands, and what permits are

needed. Unfortunately the guy staffing it just seems to turn up whenever he feels like it. It is also about 20 minutes walk from the centre.

There's another tourist office at the gate to the Secretariat, which is at the top of the hill overlooking the town. There is also a railways out-station booking office, and a Shipping Corporation of India (SCI) office there.

The post office is not far from the centre, and the telegraph office is in a wooden shack next door. Links to the mainland are unreliable. It is open from 7 am to 10 pm on weekdays, and from 8 am to 6 pm on weekends.

The SCI office is right opposite the Dhanalakshmi Hotel in Aberdeen Bazaar. Buying a ticket to Madras or Calcutta can be a real circus. First you go to this SCI office and get a piece of paper confirming that you have booked a ticket; from there you trudge up the hill to the SCI office at the Secretariat, where you pay half the fare and get another piece of paper confirming this. Then you go back to the first office in the bazaar and pay the balance, after which you might reasonably think that you would get your ticket. No, come back the next morning and it will be issued!

The Indian Airlines office is behind the post office. Flights are heavily booked and you need to have a confirmed ticket to be sure of a seat. Wait-listed passengers usually miss out.

Foreign-exchange facilities are available at banks, and there is a large regional hospital.

At 5.30 pm on Monday, Wednesday and Friday the Tourist Home has a free screening of a couple of documentary films about the islands. One is dreadful but the other is well worth seeing. The library on the same road as the post office is also a good place for information about the islands.

Cellular Jail

The main place of interest in town is the

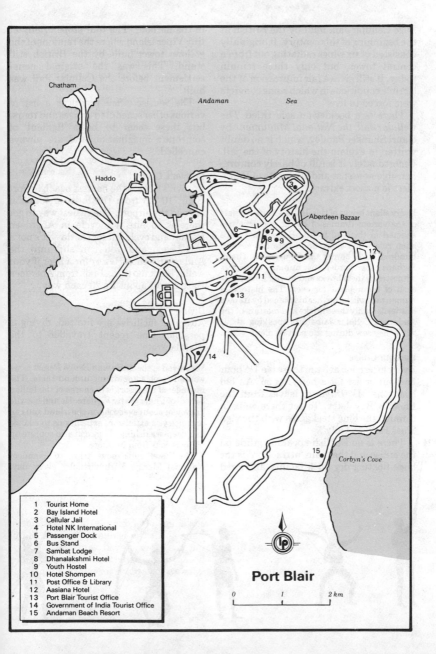

Chatham

Andaman   Sea

Haddo

Aberdeen Bazaar

Corbyn's Cove

1	Tourist Home
2	Bay Island Hotel
3	Cellular Jail
4	Hotel NK International
5	Passenger Dock
6	Bus Stand
7	Sambat Lodge
8	Dhanalakshmi Hotel
9	Youth Hostel
10	Hotel Shompen
11	Post Office & Library
12	Aasiana Hotel
13	Port Blair Tourist Office
14	Government of India Tourist Office
15	Andaman Beach Resort

Port Blair

0   1   2 km

huge Cellular Jail, built by the British at the beginning of this century. It originally consisted of six wings radiating out from a central tower, but only three remain today. It still gives a fair impression of the terrible conditions in which some convicts were forced to live.

There is a booklet on sale titled *The Cellular Jail, the National Monument* by Gauri Shanker Pandey, which is no doubt written to explain the history of the jail. Unfortunately it is full of barely comprehensible nonsense and is a waste of Rs 12. Here is a short extract:

Every silent bricks of this Jail is a mute witness of the various dramas of horror and cruelties enacted in this Jail by the British and Japs alien rulers and every brick here has several hundred such horror tales buried in them. Perhaps the burden of human sufferings witnesses by these bricks and mortar have made each of them silent for ever. The history of human race will be further blackened by its own misdeeds if only these bricks and mortars of the Andaman Cellular Jail starts speaking about what they saw during the past so many years.

Harbour Cruise

Every afternoon at 3 pm there is a 1½ hour harbour cruise for a hefty Rs 26. An old boat, the MV *Dugung*, leaves from the Phoenix Bay Jetty. To get there walk in through the blue steel gates with the sign 'Pass Holders Only'.

There is no English-speaking guide on the cruise and the main 'attraction' is the huge floating dry-dock facility anchored in the harbour. The tour stops briefly at tiny Viper Island where the remains of the gallows tower built by the British still stand. This was the original penal settlement before the Cellular Jail was built.

The tourist office produces a list of various other scheduled cruises and tours, but these seem to be a figment of someone's imagination and are always cancelled.

Corbyn's Cove

Corbyn's Cove is the nearest beach to Port Blair, 10 km from the town or four km beyond the airport. The easiest way to get there is to hire a bicycle in Aberdeen Bazaar and cycle out for the day. It's not a bad beach and you can slip into the Andaman Beach Resort for a beer if your wallet is not too thin. Taxis from Aberdeen Bazaar cost about Rs 20 each way.

Diving

Although facilities are limited, diving is possible. One recent traveller to the islands wrote:

We stayed at the *Andaman Beach Resort* as we wanted to do some diving around there. The manager of the resort is in charge of the Indian School of Under Water Welfare. He and his wife know just about everyone on the island and can organise visa extension, expeditions to islands and deep-sea fishing. They can also conjure up plane tickets from nowhere.

The hotel runs boat trips to Wandoor National Marine Park virtually every day,

although you need a minimum of four people. The trips cost about Rs 150 a shot, but give you five or six hours on an island. It's pricey but better value than trips arranged by the tourist office.

The fish and coral life are incredible. There are lots of sea snakes, turtles and dolphins to see. Anyone visiting the Andamans for diving should be aware that the best coral and visibility is at the outlying islands. Visibility is not too good off the main island. You can hire diving gear, snorkels, masks and fins. You can even organise an underwater camera for the day.

Debbie Martyr - England

Places to Stay

As the islands are mainly a tourist resort, the accommodation is geared towards this. Prices are generally higher than on the mainland, although even in season it is possible to bargain prices down quite a bit.

Places to Stay - bottom end

There are a few cheap places in Aberdeen Bazaar. The *Youth Hostel* costs round Rs 12 for a dorm bed or Rs 20 for a room. The *Sambat Lodge* is about as basic as you can get: hardboard-partitioned rooms without windows go for Rs 30. Not much better is the friendly *KK Guest House* which has tiny rooms at Rs 20/40 for singles/doubles, with common bath, although this price is definitely negotiable.

There is quite a bit of government accommodation around, but quite frankly it is so hidebound by complicated booking procedures and inconvenient locations that it's hardly worth it. The *Tourist Home* at Haddo is perhaps the only one in Port Blair worth bothering with. It is a solid 20 minute walk from the bazaar, and singles/doubles cost Rs 25/50. Food is available but the menu is limited and unexciting.

There is also the government-run *Guest House* out at Corbyn's Cove, just past the Andaman Beach Resort. It's a good place to stay but you need to check with the tourist office at the Tourist Home in Haddo to see if it's full. Rooms cost Rs 40 for a double.

Places to Stay - middle

The new *Dhanalakshmi Hotel* (tel 21306) in Aberdeen Bazaar has good singles/doubles for Rs 95/125 with attached bath; once again, you can get the price down if things are quiet. Air-con rooms cost Rs 170/200.

Another new place is the *Hotel Shompen* (tel 2948) near the Indian Airlines office. Single/double room rates are set at Rs 125/190, or Rs 190/200 with air-con. The front rooms have a balcony and views of the harbour. Bargaining is also possible here, and rates of Rs 30/50 have been reported out of season. They have a free minibus which meets all incoming flights.

On the road to Haddo, the *Hotel NK International* (tel 21066) has double rooms for Rs 125, or Rs 200 with air-con.

Places to Stay - top end

Perched on a cliff overlooking the harbour, the *Welcomgroup Bay Island Hotel* has rooms for Rs 490/610, rising to Rs 660/785 with air-con. The Bay Island has a beautiful open-air bar with great views – good for a quiet beer, although the wind usually gets up in the late afternoon.

Out at Corbyn's Cove the *Andaman Beach Resort* (tel 2599) is in a very quiet and peaceful part of the island. The off-season (May to September) rates are Rs 320/380, rising to Rs 480/570 (from mid-December to mid-February) for rooms without air-con. Meals are available and cost Rs 45 for breakfast, Rs 80 for lunch and Rs 90 for dinner; the food is apparently not all that great.

Places to Eat

The best restaurant in Port Blair is in the *Dhanalakshmi Hotel* in Aberdeen Bazaar. The food is good, the place is clean and the young owners have a good collection of music tapes. This is the place to meet other travellers in the evenings. It's open until 11 pm which is late by Port Blair standards; the streets are usually totally deserted by 9.30 pm.

After the Dhanalakshmi everything else looks extremely basic. On the ground floor of the same building, the tiny *Kattappamman Hotel* has basic vegetarian, banana-leaf thalis for Rs 5. You pay Rs 4 extra for meat, an omelette costs Rs 2.50 and you have to clean your own leaf away.

Further up the same road is the popular *Annapurna Cafe* which does good vegetarian and non-vegetarian meals. The staff are friendly and they even have a visitors' book which they'll ask you to sign!

Getting There & Away

See the Andamans Getting There & Away section for details of transport in and out of Port Blair.

Getting Around

There is a limited local bus network out of Port Blair. For getting around the town itself, or out to the beach at Corbyn's Cove, the best idea is to hire a bicycle in the bazaar. There's just one rental shop, and it takes a bit of tracking down, so ask around. It is on the same road as the bus station, just before it joins the main bazaar road.

Taxis are available for hire, either for around town or further afield.

ROSS ISLAND

This small island, which was the administrative centre in the days of the British, lies just off-shore from Port Blair. It had to be abandoned in 1941 following a serious earthquake which destroyed most of the buildings.

The government warehouses were on this island and boats were used to ferry supplies across to the main settlement.

These days Ross is returning to forest, although many ruins still remain.

Getting There & Away

Extra permits are not needed to visit the island, but you will have to charter a boat from Port Blair.

Nicobar Islands

Part of the union territory of the Andaman and Nicobar Islands, this group of 19 islands lies between the Andamans and the Indonesian island of Sumatra. It is separated from the Andamans by the 150-km-wide Ten Degree Channel.

The largest inhabited islands are Camorta and Nancowry, and the main island of the group is Car Nicobar. Seven of the islands are uninhabited.

Unfortunately the Nicobars are off limits to foreigners mainly, it seems, so that the tribal people remain undisturbed. One wonders, therefore, why Indian nationals can visit at will.

HISTORY

Like the Andamans, the Nicobar Islands were known to mariners from very early on. More recently the islands became the object of interest for missionaries keen to find new converts.

From the 17th century various European countries occupied the islands but it was the British who made the most serious attempt, taking formal control in 1869. A penal colony was also established here by the British for 20-odd years in the late 19th century.

The islands were occupied by the Japanese during WW II, but after the war were reoccupied by the Brits. In 1948 they became part of independent India.

GEOGRAPHY

With a total land area of 1953 square km the islands are generally much flatter than the Andamans, although Great Nicobar peaks at 642 metres.

CLIMATE

The climate of the Nicobars is much the same as the Andamans, with rainfall of around 3000 mm annually. The rainfall is spread throughout the year, the driest months being February, March, April and October.

The year-round temperatures vary from 18°C to 30°C.

POPULATION & PEOPLE

The Nicobarese people number about 22,000 and are thought to be a mixture of Malay and Burmese ethnic stock. They are a fair-complexioned people who have begun to adapt to contemporary Indian society. They live mainly on fish, coconuts and pigs and are organised into villages controlled by a village headman.

The Shompen are a another, much smaller, tribal group found on Great Nicobar. So far they have resisted integration into Indian society and tend to shy away from areas occupied by immigrants from the mainland, preferring to lead their lives according to their own traditions.

RELIGION

Although originally animists, the majority of Nicobarese these days have converted to Christianity and belong to the Church of India. The religion was introduced by South Indian missionaries.

GETTING THERE

Indian Airlines operates a weekly flight from Calcutta to Car Nicobar, via Port Blair in the Andaman Islands. The one-way fare from Calcutta is Rs 1555.

There is also a helicopter service connecting Car Nicobar with Port Blair. The fare is Rs 488.

Cocos (Keeling) Islands

The Cocos Islands include 27 flat coral islands in a horseshoe-shaped atoll south of Indonesia and west of Australia. Like its nearest neighbour, Christmas Island, the atoll is an Australian territory.

It is a popular stopping point for yachts sailing the Africa/Indonesia/Australia routes, but all other visitors must fly in from Perth or Christmas Island.

Facts about the Country

HISTORY

Uninhabited North Keeling Island, 24 km north of the main group, was discovered in 1609 by Captain William Keeling of the East India Company. The islands in the main atoll were also uninhabited and remained so until they were settled in 1826 by an English adventurer named Alexander Hare who brought with him his Malay harem and slaves.

A year later John Clunies-Ross, a Scots seaman, started a second settlement with his family. He began improving the natural coconut groves and brought in more Malays to help harvest the coconuts for copra. When Hare left in 1831, Clunies-Ross became the sole overlord of the islands.

The Cocos were declared a British possession in 1857 and became the responsibility of the British government in Ceylon in 1878. They were attached to the Straits Settlements in 1886 and, in the same year, Queen Victoria granted all land to the Clunies-Ross family. In 1903 the islands became part of the British crown colony of Singapore.

During WW I the German cruiser *Emden* put a raiding party on Direction Island in the north of the atoll. Soon after, in 1914, the *Emden* was destroyed by HMAS *Sydney* on the shore of North Keeling. During WW II the Japanese bombed the islands but did not occupy them.

After WW II a civil administration was appointed to the atoll, which remained part of British Singapore until it was passed to Australia.

In 1955 the Cocos Islands were accepted as a territory by Australia although a strict whites-only immigration policy by the Australian government almost stopped the transfer.

The Clunies-Ross family continued to own and run the islands until 1978 when the Australian government bought out the present John Clunies-Ross for $6.25 million. Australian currency was introduced but the new overlords began taking steps towards establishing Cocos-Malay self-government.

In 1984 the islanders were allowed to vote on 'self-determination'. Against the wishes of John Clunies-Ross, who wanted independence with Australian protectorate status, the islanders voted to remain part of Australia.

John Clunies-Ross, the fifth generation descendant of the Scottish sea captain who settled the islands, lost his millions in a failed shipping company. He moved to Perth where he was declared bankrupt, although he won a court battle with the government to keep his Great House on Home Island. His son, called Young Johnny by the islanders, still lives on Home and now leases out the family's Great House to tourists.

The atoll is now governed by an administrator who is also in charge of police, courts and immigration. The Cocos Islands Council is the local government body.

GEOGRAPHY

The Cocos Islands are 2752 km north-west of Perth and 3685 km west of Darwin. The

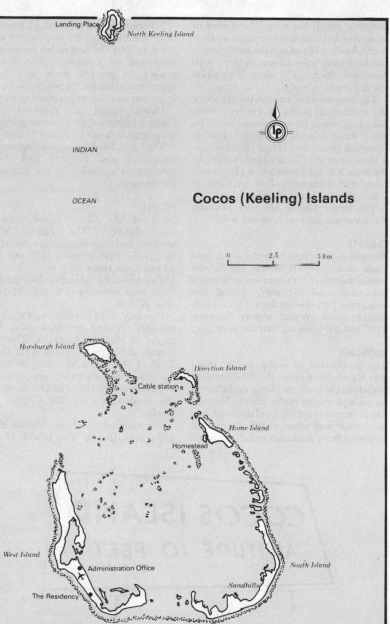

Landing Place

North Keeling Island

INDIAN

OCEAN

Cocos (Keeling) Islands

0   2.5   5 km

Horsburgh Island

Direction Island

Cable station

Home Island

Homestead

West Island

Administration Office

South Island

Sandhills

The Residency

territory, which has a total land area of 14 square km, consists two coral atolls – North Keeling Island and the main, larger southern atoll (also known as the South Keelings) which has 26 islets. Both atolls are protected by reefs.

The largest island around the lagoon of the south atoll is the 10 km long West Island on which the aerodrome lies. The other main islands are South Island, Direction Island and Home Island which is the base of the Clunies-Ross family. At the mouth of the horseshoe is Horsburgh Island and 24 km north of the main lagoon is uninhabited North Keeling Island.

The larger islands are only between three and six metres above sea level.

CLIMATE
From March to November the south-east trade winds sweep the islands. Most of the annual rainfall of 2,300 mm comes between December and February, during the 'doldrums' period when there is little wind. Temperatures remain steady between 24°C and 30°C throughout the year.

ECONOMY
The production of copra is the main activity of the Cocos, the Co-operative Society is the main employer and there is no unemployment in the islands. Enough fish is caught to satisfy local demand, but most food and other supplies must be imported from Australia and Singapore.

No-one on Cocos pays tax, all goods are duty free and there are no power or water rates. In 1984 the Australian government embarked on a A$10 million housing project to provide more and better accommodation for the islanders. In 1981 it opened an offshore quarantine station.

Meteorological data gathered in the Cocos is important for forecasting weather for a large area of the Indian Ocean.

The Cocos has its own postal service but education and medical and dental services are provided by the Australian government.

PEOPLE
Most of the Cocos inhabitants are descendants of the original Malay workers, and their dependents, brought in by Clunies-Ross between 1827 and 1831. At one time there were more than 2000 Malay-speaking islanders but most of these were resettled in Sabah, Malaysia after WW II.

Recently, with the decline of the copra industry, several hundred more have moved to Western Australia. There are now about 650 people living in the Cocos. Most of the Cocos Islanders, or Cocos-Malays as they are sometimes called, live in a kampung on Home Island, along with the descendants of the Clunies-Ross family.

The remainder of the population, about 230 people, live on West Island. Most of

COCOS ISLAND
ALTITUDE 10 FEET

these are Australians on two-year contracts, about 40 of whom work for the island's administration.

HOLIDAYS & FESTIVALS

Cocos observes the same holidays as Australia, which includes Australia Day on 26 January and Anzac Day on 25 April. The Hari Raya, the period following the Muslim fasting month of Ramadan, is also observed by the Malays.

Facts for the Visitor

VISAS

All visitors except Australian citizens require an Australian visa to visit Cocos.

GENERAL INFORMATION
Money

See the Christmas Island chapter.

Communications

The islands have their own postal service, including a philatelic bureau. Outside communication is done through the administration by radio telephone to Perth. There are no TVs or newspapers, only an island radio station.

BOOKS

Books covering the history of the Cocos Islands and the Clunies-Ross dynasty include *Kings of the Cocos* by John Scott Hughes (Methuen, London, 1950) and *Cocos Keeling: The Islands Time Forgot* by Ken Mullen (Angus & Robertson, Sydney, 1974).

HEALTH

The water supply on the islands is poor, but there's plenty of beer. Bring mosquito repellent.

ACCOMMODATION

The only official places to stay are the administration's hostel on West Island

and the Great House of the Clunies-Ross family on Home Island.

The hostel costs A$75 per day on a full-board basis or A$525 per week. To book or enquire you must contact the Indian Ocean Territories Branch in Perth. (See the Getting There & Away section for the address.)

The 100 year old Great House (sometimes called *Oceania House*) is a large, two storey manor on Home Island. Inside are teak-panelled walls and a spiral staircase leading up to the five bedrooms. Bronze busts of the Clunies-Ross generations stand guard in the hallways.

The house is leased by John Clunies-Ross to Taprobane Tours (tel 4742288), PO Box 386, Perth, WA 6100, for package tours from Perth.

The package includes flights, full-board accommodation for one week, daily diving or fishing excursions and a free bar. It costs A$1660 per person on a triple share basis, A$1710 each for a twin share or A$1910 a single. A child between two and 11 years costs A$955. Mr Clunies-Ross acts as tour guide, dive-master, boatman, you name it.

The only public bar in the Cocos Islands is the *Cocos Club* on West Island.

ACTIVITIES

Diving, snorkelling, fishing, windsurfing, surfing and swimming are your lot. Direction Island (or 'DI' as it is referred to) is the prime site for diving. (There is a monument on DI to the German raider *Emden*, destroyed by the Australians during WW I.)

The Cocos Olympics are held each October.

Getting There

An Australian Airlines 727 makes one flight per week each way between Perth and the Cocos. The return fare from Perth to Cocos and/or Christmas Island costs

A$760. The flight, every Tuesday, from Perth takes 3½ hours.

A single fare to either Cocos or Christmas island costs A$430; the fare between Cocos and Christmas costs A$140. Flights must be booked through the government's Territories Branch, Department of Arts, Sport, Environment, Tourism & Territories (tel 4811705), 6th floor, 5 Mill St, Perth, Western Australia.

The Cocos aerodrome, on West Island, is also used by Australian Air Force and US Air Force or US Navy planes – the latter usually from Diego Garcia.

There are cars and trucks on West Island. Small boats provide inter-island ferry services.

Christmas Island

A journalist who visited Christmas Island at the end of 1987, described the place an 'an amazing hybrid of an Australian mining town and a rural South-East Asian community'.

The smells of the Taoist temples and the atmosphere of Asia mix with the Holden cars, supermarket checkouts, and the beer cans littering the beauty spots. Although it's not in quite the same 'tropical paradise' league as the neighbouring Cocos Islands, Christmas Island does have some spectacular cliff scenery and, instead of being flat and coral, is high and forested.

This remote tropical territory of Australia is currently experiencing a huge cultural and economic upheaval as it endeavours to make the transition from a giant phosphate mine to an international casino resort.

The European, Chinese and Malay population is at sixes and sevens. Only the island's wildlife remains constantly rich, endearing and safe.

Christmas Island is 360 km south-west of Java, 2300 km north-west of Perth and about 850 km east of Cocos.

Facts about the Country

HISTORY

A British East India Company captain, William Mynors, gave the island its name when he spotted it on Christmas Day in 1643. The first recorded landing was made by the English navigator and part-time pirate William Dampier in March 1688.

It wasn't until near the end of the 19th century, however, that the island was found to be rich in lime phosphate, which is used as fertiliser. In June 1888 the island was declared British and later the same year George Clunies-Ross, from the Cocos

Islands, established the first settlement in Flying Fish Cove with a party of Malays. Three years later he and Sir John Murray were granted a lease to begin mining the phosphate.

In 1897 about 200 Chinese labourers, eight Europeans and five Sikh police officers arrived and the lease was taken over by the Christmas Island Phosphate Company Ltd. During WW II the island was occupied by the Japanese who, if nothing else, laid out a golf course on the terrace at Waterfall Bay in the north-east part of the island.

In 1946 Christmas Island also became part of the British colony of Singapore. Two years later the island's phosphate industry was bought jointly by Australia and New Zealand, who employed British Phosphate Commissioners (BPC) as the managing agents. The island became a crown colony on 1 January 1958 and an Australian territory nine months later, with the mining company totally owned by the government. An administrator was put in charge of the island to be responsible to the Minister for Territories.

Between 1970 and 1980 there were 3000 people on the island. The Union of Christmas Island Workers (UCIW) was formed in 1976, almost with foresight of the crisis which began the following year when the government, knowing the phosphate was running out, resettled about 1800 Asian residents in Australia.

On top of this, freight charges and production costs began to soar. The Phosphate Mining Company of Christmas Island (PMCI) was founded in 1981 to take over from the BPC. Three years later the government began to bring the island into line with the mainland, beginning by introducing income tax.

In 1985 the Christmas Island Services Corporation (CISC) was formed to take over community services, and an island

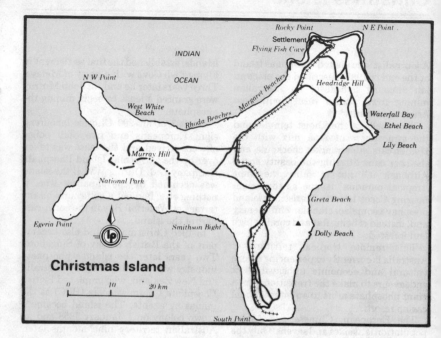

assembly was elected to take over local government. The move was made in order to get away from a 'paternalistic structure to a more democratic system'.

But the lifeblood of the island was still draining away. After a series of cutbacks in the workforce, more than 450 workers left in 1984 under a voluntary redundancy scheme. The government started looking for alternatives. The only real one was tourism, although the use of the island as a forward-defence base to replace RAAF Butterworth in Malaysia was mooted.

In 1986 the government gave the go-ahead for a A$35 million casino-resort development, work on which was due to start in late 1989.

The Australian government had said it was prepared to continue subsidising the mine operation until 1989, but a series of bans and limitations by the powerful miners' union prompted authorities to act earlier.

At the end of 1987 the government sacked the island assembly and closed the mine amidst much outcry. At one stage, extra police were sent to the island in case civil unrest broke out. Rents, electricity, water and sewerage costs had been increased, which added to the workers' ire.

The island workers continued to fight the closure, claiming mining was yet viable, but at the same time pushed for higher redundancy payments, which many of their former colleagues had already received. The workers supported the casino-resort, but saw it as only a 'life raft'. Even the future of the casino was far from certain.

The government was eventually persuaded that the phosphate mines could be reworked, but insisted on putting the contract up for tender. The island union and a Perth mining company put in a bid but the government awarded the project to the giant Elders company.

This decision, however, was overturned in court on appeal by the workers. Now they may end up back at their old jobs – and playing blackjack in the evenings

Indeed 1987 on Christmas Island was some year. Not only did the phosphate industry close down but there was the first murder trial ever held on the island. Two Chinese men were ·charged with the murder of another over a gambling win. The judge ordered that the trial be abandoned after five days, because he felt it was impossible to get an impartial jury from the island community. The men were eventually convicted in Perth in 1988.

The murder case, though, had already caused problems as it was realised that Christmas Island was still being run under British colonial laws which had operated in Singapore before WW II. Because of the absence of any serious crime, no-one had bothered to introduce modern Australian criminal legislation!

GEOGRAPHY

The triangular island is about 17 km long, 10 km across at its widest point and covers and area of 135 square km. The coastline is mostly sheer rock cliffs, and coral reefs surround the island. Within five km of the shore, the ocean floor falls away to a depth of 200 metres.

Christmas Island is the remnant of an extinct, submarine volcano which formed about 60 million years ago. As the island emerged, coral reefs formed and limestone was deposited. The island then subsided, only to re-emerge 10 million years ago in a series of uplifts which have resulted in the terraced limestone cliffs that give it a stepped appearance.

The island has risen to a height of 260 metres above sea level. Hills at the north, south and west ends surround an inland basin plateau which, millions of years ago, was a lagoon. About 14% of the island is now taken up by the open-cut phosphate mines.

Water drains quickly through the porous limestone to the harder base rock, creating many caves and sink holes. The largest cave is the one km long Lost Lake Cave, which is only accessible from the sea.

Surface water is rare, and water for domestic use is drawn from the caves and from bores into the interface between the limestone and volcanic rock.

CLIMATE

The wet season occurs between December and April when north-west monsoons bring occasional gales, heavy rain and high swells. There were bad storms in March 1988 which ripped the roofs from many homes.

From May to November the climate is 'dry'. The gentle south-east trade winds blow across the island while the north coast is sheltered and calm. Temperatures range between 22°C and 28°C throughout the year, and humidity ranges from 80% to 90%.

FLORA & FAUNA

The Christmas Island National Park takes up 12% of the island's rainforest and is set around Egeria Point in the south-west. It was set up in 1980 and is managed by the Australian National Parks & Wildlife Service. The ANPWS has a resident conservation official on the island (originally posted to ensure protection from mining operations), and there are usually visiting scientists doing research. It is proposed to extend the park to cover 65% of the island.

Flora

The island's lush rainforest has a 40 metre high canopy and little undergrowth. Crabs eat all the leaves at their level, while elsewhere great swathes have been cut through by the phosphate operations.

Although there are 21 plants endemic to the island, including native orchids and trailing hoyas, none are spectacular. There is no commercial agriculture on the island, but pawpaw and guava trees grow abundantly. The coastal vegetation is sparse; it's been reduced to saltbush and some pandanus trees.

Fauna

Christmas Island is home to thousands of birds – and 120 million crabs! The giant 'robber' or 'coconut' crab, the largest terrestrial crustacean in the world with a crushing power in its claw that is almost four times as powerful as the human jaw, is not as plentiful as the prolific red crab.

During the breeding season at the beginning of the monsoon in November, the shores are awash with swarms of red crabs heading for the sea. They descend in their millions from burrows in the rainforest. A zoologist from a Melbourne university said: 'The dramatic annual mass migration of the red crabs is one of the great sights of the natural world.' The baby crabs emerge on the shore about a month after spawning and make their way back up to the forest.

If you see a blue crab, it's a freshwater one and is protected.

Of the sea birds who congregate on Christmas Island, three are endemic to the island: the Christmas Island frigate, the beautiful golden bosun and the very rare Abbot's booby, which nests in the central-west part of the island. Of the land birds, seven species are found only on Christmas. They include the imperial pigeon, the emerald dove and the Christmas Island hawk-owl, the only endangered species.

There are few other animals or

mammals save for the large fruit bats, some feral cats and rats.

ECONOMY

The island's economy was solely based on phosphate mining until the end of 1987. The Phosphate Mining Corporation of Christmas Island employed 700 workers, members of the all-powerful Union of Christmas Island Workers led by their English general secretary Gordon Bennett. In 1979 the members staged a hunger strike to achieve parity wages with other mainland unions.

Income tax was introduced only in 1985, and is now equivalent to the full mainland rate.

The resort is hoping to attract business people from Singapore, Malaysia and Indonesia as an alternative destination to the ever-popular Bali.

PEOPLE

Of the 1100 people on the island, 66% are of Chinese descent, 12% are Malay and 22% are European. About 30% of the population are Australian citizens while the rest hold resident status.

English is the official language of the island and is taught in the schools, but most of the Chinese stick to their various dialects and the Malays use their own language.

Buddhist temples and shrines are dotted about the island and there is a mosque in the main settlement at Flying Fish Cove.

HOLIDAYS & FESTIVALS

The island's holidays and festivals are governed by Christian, Muslim and Buddhist events. Other holidays include:

Australia Day
   26 January
Anzac Day
   25 April
Queen's Birthday
   June
Territory Day
   5 October

Facts for the Visitor

VISAS

All visitors, except Australian citizens and residents, require an Australian visa to visit Christmas Island.

MONEY

The currency used on Christmas Island, and in the Cocos, is the Australian dollar, which is divided into 100 cents. There are coins of 1, 2, 5, 10, 20 and 50 cents, and $1 and $2. There are notes of $5, $10, $20, $50 and $100.

US$ 1 =	A$1.20
UK£1 =	A$2.00
C$ 1 =	A$1.08
DM 1 =	A$0.65
Fr 1 =	A$0.19
Y100 =	A$0.88

There is a Westpac bank next to the Administration building.

GENERAL INFORMATION
Post & Telecommunications

Like Cocos Island, Christmas has an autonomous postal service and issues its own stamps. The island is linked to the international telecommunications network via satellite. Telex and fax facilities are also available.

Media

There is a television service which is on the air from 3 to 11 pm during the week and longer on weekends, broadcasting taped Australian Broadcasting Commission (ABC) programmes from Perth.

The Christmas Island Services Corporation owns and runs a radio station which broadcasts in English, Malay and Mandarin. There is also a weekly newspaper, the *Christmas Island News*.

Electricity

The domestic power source is 240 volts.

Getting There

Christmas Island is serviced by the same Australian Airlines flight which goes to Cocos Island each Tuesday from Perth (see the Cocos chapter for prices).

There is also a fortnightly charter flight from Singapore, but only at certain times of the year, which costs A$600 return. The airport is currently being upgraded in the hope of increased carriers and traffic when the casino/hotel opens.

The only port is at Flying Fish Cove, the main settlement, although it is often closed to shipping because of large north-west swells running in the November-March season. Ships used to come in regularly to take away the phosphate; the giant outloading cantilever still hangs over the port. The Australian National Lines runs supply ships from Perth to the island.

Around the Island

There are five major roads, surfaced in crushed limestone, that run across the island, and there is a sealed road around the Flying Fish Cove Settlement. Many of the islanders have cars basically to save them the murderous walk up to Poon Saan and Drumsite, 200 metres higher up from the Settlement.

Visitors can hire 4WD vehicles from the Christmas Island Services Corporation (CISC) for A$62 a day.

There is also a railway running from the

cove down to the southern tip of the island but, with the closing of the mines, this is no longer used.

Flying Fish Cove

Flying Fish Cove, popularly called just 'the Cove', is the main settlement on the island and the only port.

Although enclosed by steep cliffs, it is not a particularly attractive place. It comprises a collection of differently styled housing settlements on separate levels for each ethnic community. There is a Malay kampung, a Chinese residential area known as Poon Saan, and a European area called the Settlement. Other housing areas are Silver City and Drumsite. Taman Sweetland, the former PMCI settlement, is now deserted.

The port and administration area is grouped around the cove at the lowest level, and the airport and playing fields are up on the plateau. The administrator's house is at Smith Point, south of the Cove.

Waterfall Bay

This bay on the north-east coast is the proposed site for the hotel and casino development. The golf course, not too far from Ethel and Lily beaches, is along the road to Waterfall Bay.

Walks

The island offers plenty of scope for the explorer, with scenic walks along the clifftops, through the bird colonies on the terraces and through the rainforest (see map for route).

There is also an abandoned settlement at South Point.

Beaches

Only Margaret, Rhoda and West White beaches on the north coast along from the Cove are worth visiting for the usual hedonistic pursuits, although they are hard to get to. More accessible are Greta, Dolly, Lily and Ethel beaches on the east coast. Greta Beach is the best for seeing the millions of red crabs scuttling to the seashore in November and December.

There are blowholes on the coast at Smithson Bight.

Places to Stay & Eat

There are no hotels or guest houses on the island. The 220-bed hotel and casino resort at Waterfall Bay is unlikely to be open before late 1990. Until then, the only accommodation consists of self-contained visitors' quarters provided by the CISC, the standard of which is 'very basic and limited'. A single costs about A$470 a day plus an extra A$35 for meals.

All bookings for the island must be done through The Administration for the Territory of Christmas Island, Government Offices, Christmas Island 6798, Indian Ocean.

Chinese and Malay restaurants of the formica-canteen style in the Flying Fish Cove Settlement and at Poon Saan offer a variety of Asian meals.

Activities

The two main social clubs are the Poon Saan Club, which is a Chinese gaming room, and the Christmas Island Club. There's a free open-air cinema at Poon Saan.

Settlement and Kampung in the Cove have swimming pools. There are several sporting clubs, including ones for go-karting, boating, cricket, soccer, table tennis and golf. Opportunities also arise for deep-sea fishing and diving. Contact the Christmas Island Services Corporation Community Service for details of 'What's On'.

British Indian Ocean Territory

The remote Chagos Archipelago (1000 km south of the Maldives) is all that remains of the British colonies in the Indian Ocean. The Chagos group used to be known as the Oil Islands because their only *raison d'être* was the copra industry which supplied oil to light the lamps of Port Louis, Mauritius. Now they are known as the location of Diego Garcia, the

US military base leased from the British.

Before going any further into the whys and wherefores of the Chagos, I should say that you can only travel there by private yacht. There are no civilian flights or ships into the area and the southern atoll of Diego Garcia is strictly out of bounds. To the north of the 100 km wide Great

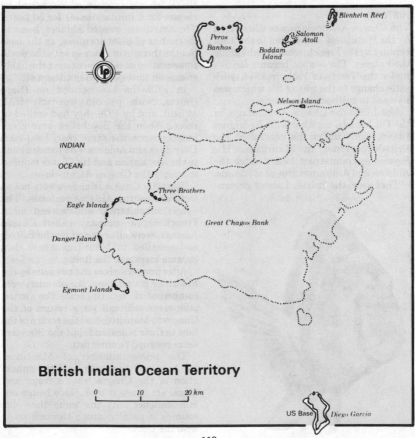

British Indian Ocean Territory

0   10   20 km

Chagos Bank are the atolls of Peros Banhos and Salomon. The other atoll, Blenheim, is more of a reef than an atoll and is uninhabitable.

Yachts and other private vessels are permitted by the British to moor and land on these atolls, but are checked over and kept under close surveillance lest they drift too close to Diego Garcia. The military personnel are reputed to be generous with their help, even to the extent of supplementing yachties' stores with the surplus of food they seem to have.

HISTORY

The Chagos Archipelago was discovered by the Portuguese and settled in the 18th century by the French, who brought along their slaves. The islands became British under the Treaty of Paris in 1814, with little change to the way of life which was devoted to cultivating coconuts.

Until 1965 the Chagos Archipelago, or the Oil Islands, together with Rodrigues Island, came under the control of the British governor in Mauritius. His Seychelles counterpart looked after the Aldabra and Amirantes groups of islands.

That year, the British Labour govern-

ment pledged the Mauritians independence and UK£3 million in compensation if they gave up their claim to the Chagos group. The deal was done.

Meanwhile, Farquhar, Desroches and Aldabra were taken away from Seychelles and, together with the Chagos group, became the British Indian Ocean Territory (BIOT). The islands came under British colonial law and used the currencies of Seychelles and Mauritius.

Behind the territorial juggling was a defence agreement with the US according to which the Americans would lease the BIOT islands (one of which would be chosen for a military base) for 50 years. The Americans wanted Aldabra, home to thousands of giant tortoises, as the base but the thought of a run-in with the world conservationist movement over the likely effects on tortoise town put them off.

In 1970 the US decided on Diego Garcia, with its old war-time RAF airfield, and by 1976 they had settled in there. When the Seychelles were given independence the same year, Farquhar, Desroches and Aldabra were handed back to the new nation and BIOT was reduced to simply the Chagos Archipelago.

The 2000 Chagos Islanders were not as fortunate as the Aldabra tortoises. The Creole inhabitants, who worked for a French copra company called Chagos Agalega, were all removed by the British and resettled in Mauritius where they became known as the Ilois.

After hunger strikes and pressure by the Mauritius government, the islanders were compensated by Britain. The leftist politicians still call for a return of the Chagos to Mauritius and the return of the Ilois to their homeland, but the islanders seem resigned to their fate.

The prime minister of Mauritius, Mr Aneerood Jugnauth, said the annexation of the Chagos was 'a fraud and illegal act, since it took place before our independence'. At the same time, his country is gaining much through trade with the USA.

BIOT is run from London by the East Africa Department of the Foreign Office. There is an administrator resident on Diego and the other islands are uninhabited.

SALOMON ATOLL

The Salomon atoll is a group of 10 islands. Only Boddam Island, at the south end of the atoll, was inhabited before the British-US clearance.

The ruins of the pier and the former settlement are still evident as are those of old homes (including the manager's chateau and the administrator's house), shops, offices, a school and a church.

The fruit trees planted by the 300 or so islanders still bear fruit regularly and the rain tanks still collect water to replenish the stores of passing yachts. Boddam is the most popular 'port' in the group for yachties. The chickens have long since run wild.

PEROS BANHOS

This is a much larger atoll about 10 km west of Salomon. On it stand similar ruins to those on Salomon.

DIEGO GARCIA

Between the northern atolls and Diego Garcia lies the Great Chagos Bank, a giant sandy and coral bank stretching 50 km from north to south and 90 km from east to west.

Diego Garcia atoll is shaped roughly like a footprint. The American forces call it the 'Footprint of Freedom', while the sailors who are posted there refer to it as 'The Rock'.

The atoll, as well as producing copra, was a coaling station for ships crossing the Indian Ocean. The *Lusitania* was one of its more famous customers. Now it is base to a classified number of American servicemen (estimated at 3000) who are subject to British laws. An administrator is in charge of the atoll and is supported by a small Royal Navy detachment, a magistrate, doctor, some clerks and a few policemen.

The base, on the north-west end of the atoll, has cinemas, shops, bars, a Kentucky Fried Chicken outlet and all the trappings of hometown America. It also has, in varying numbers and at varying times, battle cruisers, submarines, supply ships, tankers, bombers, fighters, reconnaissance aircraft and the full support facilities necessary for the use of the Rapid Deployment Joint Task.

At the other end of the atoll is the village of the former inhabitants, now a ghost town. In between, stretches the base's runway which is three km long.

Lakshadweep Islands

Known as the Laccadive Islands until 1973, the Lakshadweeps lie in the Arabian Sea off the coast of Kerala, in south-west India, and are a northern extension of the Maldives. The name means '100,000 islands'; a slight misnomer as there are in fact only 34 of them, 12 of which are coral atolls.

The Lakshadweeps are open only to organised groups and the tourism possibilities for foreigners are limited to one of the uninhabited islands, Bangaram. Indian nationals, however, can visit other islands as well.

HISTORY
In the 11th century an Arab scholar split the archipelago into the Maldives and the Laccadives. The islanders were later converted to Islam. In the 15th century the Portuguese moved in and built forts, although they were evicted by the local inhabitants only half a century later. The islands became a dependent state of the Raja of Cannanore (in Kerala) in the 16th century, and were finally taken over by the British in 1877.

In 1948 the Lakshadweep Islands, like the Andamans and Nicobars, became a union territory of the Republic of India.

CLIMATE
The average minimum daily temperature is 24°C, the maximum 31°C. The best time for a visit is from mid-September to mid-May.

POPULATION & PEOPLE
The people of the Lakshadweep, the Moplahs, are of mixed Arab and Indian descent and number about 42,000. The majority speak Malayalam, a Keralan (Indian) language, but use Arabic script for the written form of the language. However the people on the largest island,

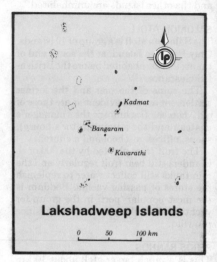

Minocy, speak an ancient form of Sinhala known as Mahl.

The main activities are the manufacture of coconut husk fibre, fishing and boat building.

PERMITS
Foreign tourists need permits to visit the Lakshadweep Islands. These are generally only issued if you are joining a package tour, and are only valid for the uninhabited island of Bangaram.

Permits are available from the Administrator (tel 69131), Union Territory of Lakshadweep, Indira Gandhi Rd, Willingdon Island, Cochin. Four passport photos are needed.

ACCOMMODATION
On Bangaram there are eight 'family huts' available for Rs 80 per day. For Indian nationals there are three similar huts on Kavarathi and 10 'honeymoon

huts' on Kadmat; these islands are closed to foreigners.

The all-inclusive price of the seven day tour from Cochin is Rs 1290 deck class, and Rs 1440 in a two-berth air-con cabin.

GETTING THERE & AWAY

The Shipping Corporation of India vessel, the MV *Bharatseema*, makes the trip to and from the islands three to five times a month. In India the vessel departs from Cochin in Kerala and the trip takes about 18 hours. Passengers should be prepared for rough seas.

Index

124

MAPS

Temperature

To convert °C to °F multiply by 1.8 and add 32

To convert °F to °C subtract 32 and multiply by ·55

Length, Distance & Area

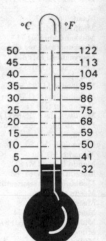

	multiply by
inches to centimetres	2.54
centimetres to inches	0.39
feet to metres	0.30
metres to feet	3.28
yards to metres	0.91
metres to yards	1.09
miles to kilometres	1.61
kilometres to miles	0.62
acres to hectares	0.40
hectares to acres	2.47

Weight

	multiply by
ounces to grams	28.35
grams to ounces	0.035
pounds to kilograms	0.45
kilograms to pounds	2.21
British tons to kilograms	1016
US tons to kilograms	907

A British ton is 2240 lbs, a US ton is 2000 lbs

Volume

	multiply by
Imperial gallons to litres	4.55
litres to imperial gallons	0.22
US gallons to litres	3.79
litres to US gallons	0.26

5 imperial gallons equals 6 US gallons
a litre is slightly more than a US quart, slightly less
than a British one

Other guides to Islands of the Indian Ocean

Madagascar & the Comoros - a travel survival kit
Despite its proximity to Africa, Madagascar's flora and
fauna are unique - lemurs are the best-known example -
and it was first settled by Indonesians. It is the fourth
largest island in the world, with a vibrant mix of cultures
and unusual landscapes. The tiny, volcanic Comoros
offer adventurous travellers the experience of a
lifetime.

Mauritius, Réunion & the Seychelles -
a travel survival kit
Mauritius is a strange blend of Indian, Creole and French
cultures - and travel is cheap. Réunion is France's best-
kept secret - a superb volcanic island and one of its last
colonies. The Seychelles have been discovered by divers,
climbers - and beach lovers.

Guides to West Asia

Bangladesh - a travel survival kit
The adventurous traveller in Bangladesh can explore
tropical forests and beaches, superb hill country, and
ancient Buddhist ruins. This guide covers all these
alternatives - and many more.

India - a travel survival kit
An award-winning guidebook that is recognised as the
outstanding contemporary guide to the subcontinent.
Looking for a houseboat in Kashmir? Trying to post a
parcel? This definitive guidebook has all the facts.

Kashmir, Ladakh & Zanskar - a travel survival kit
This book contains detailed information on three
contrasting Himalayan regions in the Indian state of
Jammu and Kashmir - the narrow valley of Zanskar,
reclusive Ladakh, and the beautiful Vale of Kashmir.

Kathmandu & the Kingdom of Nepal
   – a travel survival kit
Few travellers can resist the lure of magical Kathmandu and its surrounding mountains. This guidebook takes you round the temples, to the foothills of the Himalaya, and to the Terai.

Pakistan – a travel survival kit
Pakistan has been called 'the unknown land of the Indus' and many people don't realise the great variety of experiences it offers – from bustling Karachi, to ancient cities and tranquil mountain valleys.

Sri Lanka – a travel survival kit
This guide takes a complete look at the island Marco Polo described as 'the finest in the world'. In one handy package you'll find ancient cities, superb countryside, and beautiful beaches.

Turkey – a travel survival kit
Historic Turkey, bridging Asia and Europe, offers a wide range of travel experiences – from the excitement of Istanbul's bazaars to Mediterranean beaches and remote mountains. This widely acclaimed book has all the facts.

West Asia on a shoestring
A complete guide to the overland trip from Bangladesh to Turkey. Updated information on Bangladesh, Bhutan, India, Iran, Maldives, Nepal, Pakistan, Sri Lanka, Turkey and the Middle East, even Afghanistan as it used to be!

Also Available:
Hindi/Urdu phrasebook, *Nepali phrasebook* and *Sri Lanka phrasebook*

Lonely Planet Guidebooks

Lonely Planet guidebooks cover virtually every accessible part of Asia as well as Australia, the Pacific, Central and South America, Africa, the Middle East and parts of North America. There are four main series: 'travel survival kits', covering a single country for a range of budgets; 'shoestring' guides with compact information for low-budget travel in a major region; trekking guides; and 'phrasebooks'.

Mail Order

Lonely Planet guidebooks are distributed worldwide and are sold by good bookshops everywhere. They are also available by mail order from Lonely Planet, so if you have difficulty finding a title please write to us. US and Canadian residents should write to Embarcadero West, 112 Linden St, Oakland CA 94607, USA and residents of other countries to PO Box 617, Hawthorn, Victoria 3122, Australia.

Lonely Planet

Lonely Planet published its first book in 1973. Tony and Maureen Wheeler had made a lengthy overland trip from England to Australia and, in response to numerous 'how do you do it?' questions, Tony wrote and they published *Across Asia on the Cheap*. It became an instant local best-seller and inspired thoughts of a second travel guide. A year and a half in South-East Asia resulted in their second book, *South-East Asia on a Shoestring*, which they put together in a backstreet Chinese hotel in Singapore in 1975. The 'yellow book', as it quickly became known, soon became *the* guide to the region and has gone through five editions, always with its familiar yellow cover.

Soon other writers came to them with ideas for similar books – books that went off the beaten track with an adventurous approach to travel, books that 'assumed you knew how to get your luggage off the carousel,' as one reviewer put it. Lonely Planet grew from a kitchen table operation to a spare room and then to its own office. Its international reputation began to grow as the Lonely Planet logo began to appear in more and more countries. In 1982 *India – a travel survival kit* won the Thomas Cook award for the best guidebook of the year.

These days there are over 70 Lonely Planet titles. Over 40 people work at our office in Melbourne, Australia and another half dozen at our US office in Oakland, California.

At first Lonely Planet specialised in the Asia region but these days we are also developing major ranges of guidebooks to the Pacific region, to South America and to Africa. The list of walking guides is growing and Lonely Planet now has a unique series of phrasebooks to 'unusual' languages. The emphasis continues to be on travel for travellers and Tony and Maureen still manage to fit in a number of trips each year and play a very active part in the writing and updating of Lonely Planet's guides.

Keeping guidebooks up to date is a constant battle which requires an ear to the ground and lots of walking, but technology also plays its part. All Lonely Planet guidebooks are now stored and updated on computer, and some authors even take lap-top computers into the field. Lonely Planet is also using computers to draw maps and eventually many of the maps will be stored on disk.

The people at Lonely Planet strongly feel that travellers can make a positive contribution to the countries they visit both by better appreciation of cultures and by the money they spend. In addition the company tries to make a direct contribution to the countries and regions it covers. Since 1986 a percentage of the income from each book has gone to aid groups and associations. This has included donations to famine relief in Africa, to aid projects in India, to agricultural projects in Central America, to Greenpeace's efforts to halt French nuclear testing in the Pacific and to Amnesty International. In 1989 $41,000 was donated by Lonely Planet to these projects.

Lonely Planet Distributors

Australia & Papua New Guinea Lonely Planet Publications, PO Box 617, Hawthorn, Victoria 3122.
Canada Raincoast Books, 112 East 3rd Avenue, Vancouver, British Columbia V5T 1C8.
Denmark, Finland & Norway Scanvik Books aps, Store Kongensgade 59 A, DK-1264 Copenhagen K.
India & Nepal UBS Distributors, 5 Ansari Rd, New Delhi – 110002
Israel Geographical Tours Ltd, 8 Tverya St, Tel Aviv 63144.
Japan Intercontinental Marketing Corp, IPO Box 5056, Tokyo 100-31.
Kenya Westland Sundries Ltd, PO Box 14107, Nairobi, Kenya.
Netherlands Nilsson & Lamm bv, Postbus 195, Pampuslaan 212, 1380 AD Weesp.
New Zealand Transworld Publishers, PO Box 83-094, Edmonton PO, Auckland.
Singapore & Malaysia MPH Distributors, 601 Sims Drive, #03-21, Singapore 1438.
Spain Altair, Balmes 69, 08007 Barcelona.
Sweden Esselte Kartcentrum AB, Vasagatan 16, S-111 20 Stockholm.
Thailand Chalermnit, 108 Sukhumvit 53, Bangkok 10110.
Turkey Yab-Yay Dagitim, Alay Koshu Caddesi 12/A, Kat 4 no. 11-12, Cagaloglu, Istanbul.
UK Roger Lascelles, 47 York Rd, Brentford, Middlesex, TW8 0QP
USA Lonely Planet Publications, PO Box 2001A, Berkeley, CA 94702.
West Germany Buchvertrieb Gerda Schettler, Postfach 64, D3415 Hattorf a H.
All Other Countries refer to Australia address.